# NET PROMOTER®
## IMPLEMENT THE SYSTEM

By Maurice FitzGerald B.E.
With Peter FitzGerald D.Phil.

D1509585

# Copyright

Published in Switzerland
First edition, 2017

ISBN 978-2-9701172-4-7

Maurice FitzGerald Consulting
Chemin des Crêts-de-Champel
1206 Geneva
Switzerland
www.customerstrategy.net

# About the authors

Maurice FitzGerald

Maurice retired from Hewlett Packard Enterprise where he was Vice-President of Customer Experience for Software up to early 2016. Before moving to HP Software in 2012, Maurice spent six years as a member of both the overall HP EMEA Leadership Team and the EMEA Enterprise Business Management Team. He implemented HP strategies that cross all businesses and functions, with a special focus improving Enterprise customer experience with HP. Other work included business strategy development for emerging markets, vertical industries, and a variety of transformational initiatives particularly in sales. He led the EDS / HP integration work for the Enterprise Business in Europe the Middle East and Africa. He has also worked for Compaq, Digital Equipment Corporation, and Blue Bell Apparel, the parent company of Wrangler jeans at the time.

Peter FitzGerald

After his Bachelor's degree in Psychology from the National University of Ireland, Peter went on to do his doctorate in Cognitive Psychology at Oxford University. Among the important things he learned was that he needed to paint with his left hand, rather than his right. He combined early work at the Max Planck Institute in Munich with the development of a successful career as an artist. He ultimately left psychology to work in the visual arts full-time, including thirteen years as the editor-in-chief of Ireland's leading art magazine, *Circa*. In addition to artwork, Peter also designs and implements websites and newsletters for galleries and other businesses. His website is at iCulture.website.

# Acknowledgments

The last nine months spent writing this book and its two companion titles have been a fantastic learning experience. I learned how to transfer knowledge from my brain to my writing software. I also learned there is broad interest in my chosen subjects.

There are several people whom I must thank for their help and guidance.

First, of course, is my brother who did all the line drawings in all three books. His artistic ability and wry sense of humor come across well. Peter's years of professional experience as the editor of Ireland's leading art magazine, CIRCA, have also been invaluable. His eagle eye caught many mistakes I would never have seen, no matter how often I read the books out loud to myself.

Our test readers provided hundreds of improvement suggestions. I particularly want to thank Alyona Medelyan, Lindsay Hall, my sisters Una and Claire, Lena Palombo Forssell, Luc Vanden Plas, Matti Airas, François Gschwindemann, Michelle Tom, and David Jacques. Dale Halvorson, Dr. James Borderick and Ian Maddrell also provided much-needed encouragement and indeed stimulation to start writing in the first place.

And I can't forget my daughter Claire's great work on the cover illustrations. She, her sister Michelle and my wife Danielle have provided the support I need on the journey so far.

# Contents

# It started in a bathtub

I suppose it all started in a bathtub in 1981. I was working for the Wrangler jeans company in Paris. My boss was in his bathtub. (I hasten to add that I was not present at the time.) We had a line of 'shrink to fit' jeans. The idea was that you would get into a hot bath with the new jeans, soak for a while, and they would shrink 12% to fit your body perfectly. In the trade, we called these 'spray on jeans'. The target market was of course shapely young women. While my boss was waiting, he played around with a pumice stone, rubbing on the jeans. He liked what he saw, went out and bought all the pumice stones he could find, and destroyed his home washing machine trying out his idea. In short, he was one of a number of people at the origin of high-volume stonewashing of jeans. I was his quality and engineering manager and he told me to make this into a high-volume commercial process. While that would be a story in itself, what is relevant here is what happened when I decided to ask our customers what they actually wanted. It was not at all what we expected.

Since nobody had ever gone out and asked store owners for their opinions in a formal way, I consulted with my corporate colleagues first. My HQ friends in Greensboro, North Carolina were sure the store owners would mainly have huge concerns about how stonewashing was destroying the stitching, weakening the fabric, damaging the rivets and so on. Others thought the input would be around the accuracy of order picking. Still others were certain the jeans would be ignored and that all the input would be about the new line of shirts. Overall, the message I received loud and clear was "Don't waste your time asking. We already know what the customers want." They were all wrong. Since I believed what they said, I was wrong too.

One of the sales people was enthusiastic about the survey, so we went ahead, despite the input from my colleagues. I also ignored advice to ask a series of detailed question about the stitching, rivets and so on, and just went out with a few open questions. We visited the major boutiques in Paris and got a lot of surprises. The most important thing by far to them was that we should deliver all goods during the half-day we promised. It turned out that they would arrange for family and friends to come over to help unload the cartons and put things on the shelves. Order picking accuracy did not matter much. They were happy to put whatever they received on the shelves and try to sell it over the weekend, returning it on the Monday if we had made a mistake. The quality of the fabric, stitching, zips and rivets was never mentioned. The uniformity of stonewashing mattered a lot. "We get women who want the look they see in a jean that is not available in their size. You really need to make the stonewashing more uniform, so it looks the same in all sizes."

In short, none of the top five priorities were on the list of what we expected.

I regret to say that the main reaction of the HQ people was "That's just those crazy French people. You shouldn't pay any attention to what they say." Locally, we implemented a plan to improve the main things they suggested. It worked, and we retained leadership over Levis, Lois and Lee. Thanks to David Hayes for the leadership.

The message here is not about jeans or Parisian clothing stores. The message is that if you believe you know what your customers want, but have not actually asked them, you are probably wrong.

# 1. Introduction to NPS

# 1.1   What is this book about?

The Net Promoter System[®1] is the most widely adopted system for managing customer feedback and improvement. It is used around the world and works well in all cultures and languages. Like most management systems, it has advantages and disadvantages. Its principal advantage is its simplicity. It is easy to understand and easy to communicate. Its disadvantages are two-fold: its lack of sophistication means it is tempting to find more intellectually pleasing solutions, and many implementers confuse the Net Promoter Score[®] and the Net Promoter System. Before going into detail on NPS[®], let's cover a few important points.

### Current state of customer feedback systems on planet Earth

Like most readers, I receive requests to take surveys almost every day. Since I am interested in the topic, I fill out a lot of survey forms. I almost never hear anything from the people who sent the survey after that. What have they learned? What are they doing with my input. I took fifteen minutes to answer their questions, why can't they take two minutes to keep me informed? Maybe they had no plans to do anything with the input other than report numbers to their management? Six months or a year later, I can observe that none of my improvement suggestions have been put into practice. I wind up feeling that my time has been wasted, and theirs too, since no action seems to have been taken.

This book is about eliminating that waste, moving from survey processes to a mutual feedback and improvement process. The content builds on the author's experience in implementing the Net Promoter System at HP, and helping others to do the same. While the system set out by Fred Reichheld and Rob Markey in *The Ultimate Question 2.0*[2] serves as the basis for all

---

[1]   Net Promoter, Net Promoter System, Net Promoter Score, NPS and the NPS-related emoticons are registered trademarks of Bain & Company, Inc., Fred Reichheld and Satmetrix Systems, Inc.

[2]   Fred Reichheld with Rob Markey: *The Ultimate Question 2.0*, Harvard Business Review Press, 2011, ISBN 978-1-4221-7335-0

that follows, the system has been augmented in several ways that should speed up both implementation and results.

Do I actually need a feedback and improvement system?

Maybe you don't absolutely need one. If you have a monopoly in your market and have government-imposed pricing, there may be nothing to gain in the short term. Why spend money if you already have all the income you can possibly get? Of course, your monopoly may not last. As well-known strategy guru Willie Pietersen told my class at Columbia Business School, "Somewhere in the world, somebody has just had an idea that will destroy your business."

Cable TV companies discovered this to their cost when telcos started to compete with them. Most businesses are not monopolies and care about winning in their markets. They care about growth. According to Bain and Satmetrix, co-holders of the NPS service mark, NPS trends predict 20 to 60% of business growth[3] trends, depending on the industry. Understanding how happy your customers are compared to your competitors is usually at least as important as comparing your sales coverage models and product features.

---

[3]  http://www.netpromotersystem.com/about/how-is-nps-related-to-growth.aspx

# What is this book about?

Make sure your customers are a company priority

Rather than reacting by saying "Of course we care about customers!" check your intranet, corporate annual reports, press releases and quarterly earnings statements. Do they actually mention customers? Check your CEO's latest motivational email to all employees. Are customers mentioned in the top three priorities? Is cost reduction above customers on the priority list? Are things like "It is critical that we deliver the current quarter" at the top of the list? Checking the evidence is easy enough. It allows you to determine whether your company cares about customers from a strategic perspective. If customers are close to the top of the formal priority list in your company at the moment, get formal sponsorship for your NPS work and move ahead. More on how to get sponsorship this in a later chapter. If customers are not on the list, you have some persuasion work to do first, and we will discuss how to do it.

Use operational data, not NPS, to run your company daily

All companies use operational data to ensure their processes are working as designed. The processes are in turn designed to maximize revenue, optimize cost, and respect defined service levels. Many operational metrics are delivered in real time. NPS has a time lag. Customer research and feedback needs to be used to adjust, prioritize and improve operational metrics. It is also particularly useful for the study of the relationship between cost and growth. For example, you may be able to show that pursuit of a particular cost metric has a measurable positive or negative effect on NPS, and therefore on future revenue.

In many cases, business processes that are cheap and simple are better for customers, as they may be faster and more efficient for them too. Operational data often has gaps or "white space". This means your operational data may look good while the customer feedback may be bad. The most common example of this is the difference between the way customers measure delivery time for their orders compared to the way companies measure it. This will be covered in more detail later. NPS should be used to supplement, correct and prioritize operational metrics, not as a substitute.

# Introduction

Avoid common mistakes

Customers are important to your company. Implementing a feedback system will improve their lives and your financial results. This book will speed up your NPS work and will help you avoid many common implementation mistakes. You will benefit from understanding mistakes made by the author and others, and how they can be addressed or avoided.

Contents

The book is divided into the following sections:

- Refresher on the history and main aspects of the Net Promoter System.
- Ensuring NPS is a reliable, trusted metric.
- Feedback, learning and improvement processes — the heart of the system.
- Implementing a robust operational and analytic infrastructure.
- An employee and team environment focused on loyalty.
- Ensuring sustained leadership commitment.

Real-life examples of how to implement well and how to fail are provided throughout the book.

# 1.2   Net Promoter System history

This book supposes the reader is already familiar with the basics of the Net Promoter System, and ideally has read *The Ultimate Question 2.0* by Fred Reichheld and Rob Markey. There is quite a lot of mis-information about what they wrote. Some comes from people who have not read the book. Some comes from people who have read it, but had difficulty understanding some points. I have had the opportunity to clarify a few tricky points directly with the source. Let's start with the metric, rather than the overall system. Exhibit 1.1 shows how the scoring works.

**Exhibit 1.1**

NPS rating question and scale

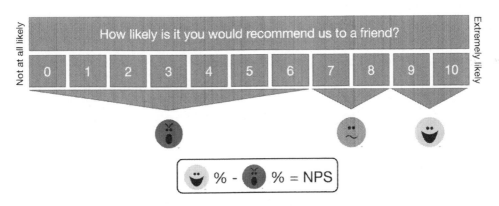

Open questions
After the rating question, the current standard is to use two open questions:

1. Why?
2. What should we improve?

Additional questions may be used for touchpoint surveys, also called 'experience surveys' or 'interaction surveys'.

# Introduction

## Which direction for the scale?
Fred and Rob have used the scale in both directions, from zero to 10 and the opposite. There are views, supported by psychology experiments, that the order biases the results in one direction or the other. It does not matter which you use, as long as you are consistent. Personally, I have always used it as shown here, though I agreed to requests to reverse the scale from my HP colleagues in countries that write from right to left to reverse the scale.

## What about using a different scale?
Some companies use a 1 to 5 scale, with 5 as the best score and the only Promoter score. 4 is for Passives and 1 to 3 for Detractors. This has two disadvantages. First, all too many people believe they should strive to be number 1, and therefore think that 1 is the top score, no matter how it is labeled. This is quite easy to spot if you also have an open text question and the answer seems opposite to the rating, though the respondent could be trying to be sarcastic. Second, there are cultures that just don't want to give you the top score. On a scale from 0 to 10, the happiest people in these cultures may give you a 9, but on a 1 to 5 scale they give you a 4.

Again, all this does not matter much if you are consistent, only comparing yourself with others using the same scale. When HP moved from the short to the long scale for competitive benchmark surveys, Satmetrix advised that it would have a small positive effect on NPS scores for HP and for all competitors. That is indeed what happened.

## Your ultimate question may not be the recommendation question
This may seem subtle: when Fred wrote the original Harvard Business Review paper, *The One Number You Need to Grow*[4], he found that the recommendation question trend was the best revenue predictor for most but not all industries. This matters. Your personal 'Ultimate question' should be whatever single question best predicts your revenue and market share trends relative to your competition. You should start by using the

---

[4] The "One Number You Need to Grow" HRB article can be found here:
https://hbr.org/2003/12/the-one-number-you-need-to-grow

recommendation question in the absence of any contrary data. Even in industries where it was not the best question, it was close to the top.

I realize this statement is somewhat controversial. Fred and Rob have stated it publicly in Episode 82 of the Net Promoter System Podcast series[5]. Some of their early work, notably with Enterprise Rent-A-Car, did not use the recommendation question. There are limits to what you should use, to avoid confusion. First, you will cause confusion if you let each business and function in your company select their own question and all refer to it as NPS. You can only have a single question formulation in your company if you want to be able to communicate effectively. Second, don't allow composite metrics made up from multiple questions to be represented as NPS. That is opposite to the whole principle of a single simple question.

## Categories and behaviors
From the start, the Bain teams were able to observe and quantify behavior by response category. I suppose the most important observation is that a 5 is absolutely not a middle-of-the-road average score. People who give you a 5 (on the 0 to 10 scale) do not like you and may well speak negatively about you to others. The same applies to those who give you a 3 on a 1-to-5 scale. This is an important observation when thinking about how people use Customer Satisfaction (CSAT) scores on a five-point scale. CSAT practitioners consider people who give a 3 to be satisfied, and they are not. Their actions say otherwise.

## Early research with Satmetrix
Bain asked Satmetrix to provide additional proof that NPS trends relative to competitors correspond to relative revenue growth, expressed as a percentage. This applied once again to most but not all industries studied. The main exceptions were industries that tend to have local monopolies, such as cable television companies. Fred found the relationship between NPS trends and relative growth to be particularly striking in the airline industry. In the HBR article referred to above, he says "… no airline has

---

[5]   All podcasts are at http://www.netpromotersystem.com/resources/podcast.aspx

found a way to increase growth without improving its ratio of promoters to detractors."

## Don't forget common sense
Accept for a moment that the recommendation question is the best one-question growth and share predictor for your company. Imagine you have seen multiple quarters of positive NPS trends relative to your competition. Growth ahead! What could possibly go wrong? Many things. Let's suppose you run a software business that is entirely dependent on sales people that go to visit customers and that you have no intention of changing that. Each sales person has an average quota for the industry of about $2 million per year. You decide that you can't afford to hire any additional sales people. Happier customers may make it easier for the existing sales people to make their quotas and will renew more of their existing annual contracts, but you will be throwing away the full growth opportunity if you don't hire more sales people.

To use a non-NPS example, warmer weather predicts improved ice cream sales. If you don't have additional ice cream in stock, you won't sell any more. A Net Promoter System that functions well and produces better scores is simply a business enabler. You still have to convert the opportunity it creates.

## Analyzing text responses
Humans are unfortunately subject to all sorts of cognitive biases. These are problematic when it comes to the search for insights in customer responses to the open Why and Improve questions. Consciously or unconsciously, we all tend to see things we already believe or agree with more quickly than we recognize things we don't particularly care to see. Unless you have only a small number of verbatim responses, software will be an invaluable aid to your search for new insights. There were no good solutions available when Fred and Rob wrote their book. That has changed, and we will cover how to evaluate survey analysis software. As it exists today, software can do an excellent job of initial screening and categorization, and humans still control the final decisions.

## The books

Fred Reichheld published *The Ultimate Question* in March 2006. Rob Markey co-wrote the 'revised and expanded' v2.0 of the book and published it in September 2011. As of July 2017, they do not yet plan to write v3.0. Nevertheless, their methodology has been improving since 2011. The updates are reasonably clear in certain *Bain Net Promoter System Podcasts*, specifically the ones where Rob Markey speaks on his own, or together with Fred. Rob and I also recorded a podcast together in July 2017 and clarified many of the improvements to the system.

To me, the single most important change is the addition of a third question to the prior standard set of two, "What would you like us to improve?" The reason it matters is that the old standard meant that Detractors gave clear suggestions for improvement, but Promoters did not get that opportunity. Promoters generally love you and want to help. They give longer and more helpful improvement suggestions than Detractors. The current standard is a three-question format for most surveys. Transactional surveys may include one or two additional questions, as we will see later.

# 1.3 Framework

The Bain & Company Net Promoter System Framework has five elements, as shown in Exhibit 1.2 This book discusses how to implement each element.

### Exhibit 1.2

Bain Net Promoter System framework

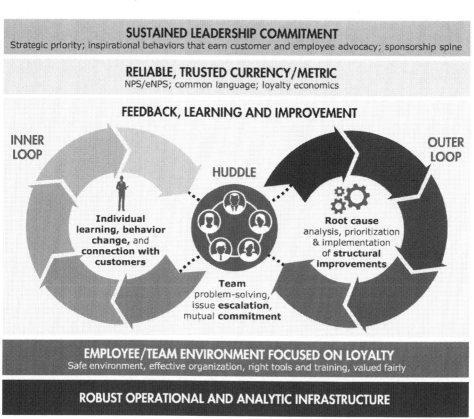

SUSTAINED LEADERSHIP COMMITMENT
Strategic priority; inspirational behaviors that earn customer and employee advocacy; sponsorship spine

RELIABLE, TRUSTED CURRENCY/METRIC
NPS/eNPS; common language; loyalty economics

FEEDBACK, LEARNING AND IMPROVEMENT

INNER LOOP

OUTER LOOP

HUDDLE

Individual learning, behavior change, and connection with customers

Root cause analysis, prioritization & implementation of structural improvements

Team problem-solving, issue escalation, mutual commitment

EMPLOYEE/TEAM ENVIRONMENT FOCUSED ON LOYALTY
Safe environment, effective organization, right tools and training, valued fairly

ROBUST OPERATIONAL AND ANALYTIC INFRASTRUCTURE

# Framework

The material on some parts of the framework is more detailed than others, notably everything that is involved in ensuring NPS is a reliable and trusted metric in your organization. It is unlikely that the system can be implemented by consensus. Attempts to get everyone possible to agree to what needs to be done will lead to excessive complexity, and lack of clarity about the priorities. Personal leadership is required, and it can only be completely successful in the context of sustained commitment from senior leaders. The chapters on each part of the framework include examples of good practice. Real-world counter-examples are provided between the framework chapters. There is somewhat of a theme in the counter-examples: excessive focus on metrics, rather than improvement. We will start by discussing how to ensure NPS is a 'reliable, trusted currency/metric', work down the framework, and finish by covering leadership commitment.

## 1.4  Learning check

Decide whether each of these statements is true or false. Answers are at the back of the book.

1. The answers to "How likely are you to recommend [Company] to a friend?" were found to be the best predictors of future revenue trends among all the questions tested by Fred Reichheld in his 2003 Harvard Business Review article *The One Number You Need to Grow*.
2. The answers to the "How likely are you to recommend [Company] to a friend?" were found to be the best growth predictors for all industries tested, in the same HBR article.
3. The Net Promoter Score scale must start at zero and go to ten. All other scales are invalid.
4. Reichheld's research showed that customer behaviors really do change depending on their classification as Promoters, Passives or Detractors.
5. The definitive reference source for the Net Promoter System is *The Ultimate Question 2.0*, and no other information on the design and implementation is available from Reichheld and Markey.

# 2. Reliable, trusted metric - Part 1

## 2.1  Purpose

The Net Promoter System relies on a metric that is easy to understand, and perhaps paradoxically, easy to misunderstand or even deliberately misuse. There are several different ways of generating a Net Promoter Score. Each has its own specific use. Each is reliable in a different way. It is quite common to see companies advance marketing statements like "Our NPS is 92, with a 30-point lead over our nearest competitor." No explanation is typically provided about where the number comes from. I have investigated a number of such claims in detail. Typically, the two numbers being compared are from different types of surveys, and are not actually comparable.

This part of the book is about how to ensure both a reliable score and a trusted feedback-gathering process. The trust has internal and external aspects. Internally, your colleagues must believe that the feedback is indeed representative of the customer and competitor base it claims to represent. Externally, your feedback and improvement process must provide more value to customers than it extracts. If not, fewer customers will respond to your next feedback request, decreasing reliability.

Making it matter as much as financial metrics
You want NPS to be included in leadership team discussions and to have similar status to any other robust metric, such as your P&L. You need to be able to report your key research results with the same frequency and reliability. If your main financial discussions are quarterly, your main NPS reports should be quarterly too. Just as your P&L is compared to that of your competition, your NPS report should include competitive information as well. Competitive benchmark surveys are covered in the next chapter.

NPS feedback needs to represent your customer population
Assuming you are not wasting your customers' time and are going to act, you need to ensure your feedback is representative. The purpose of the

whole system is to improve loyalty and encourage customers to promote you to others. You need to be clear which customers this means and to target them correctly in any feedback system. To pick an example, if you want to get feedback about your product, but only use data about people who contact you with problems, your feedback system is incomplete at best. Let me pick an extreme example in another domain to illustrate this. For many years, homosexuality was on the formal US list of psychiatric illnesses. Research by psychiatrists showed that gay people had a truly amazing set of symptoms. The root cause of this classification problem was that the only homosexuals psychiatrists studied were people who had been referred to them because they had psychiatric illnesses. It took many years before this was understood and corrected.

### Types of NPS research

The conventional types of feedback scores and input you need to understand and be able to use are benchmark and supplier surveys, relationship feedback, product / service / project feedback, transactional feedback and the feedback from your own employees, known as eNPS. Each can help you to understand and predict different things. They should never be mixed together or compared to each other. Each needs to be reliable and trusted in its own way.

### Introducing a new type of research: 'ceNPS'

I will cover eNPS in the section about ensuring you have an Employee / Team environment focused on loyalty. At that point, I will introduce a new type of research, which is called customer-employee NPS. The principle is that you ask your own employees how likely customers are to recommend your company, why, and what should be improved. This can be valuable in addition to customer research because employees are better positioned than customers to understand which improvements are easy to implement.

## 2.2 Competitive benchmarks and supplier surveys

Quite a few companies sell NPS benchmark data. Some will do custom surveys to your design. Done properly, benchmark survey trends are the best predictor of revenue and market share trends for your company. Since benchmark surveys provide comparative data, they are actually the only credible predictors. All other survey types cover only your company. Feedback about your product may be improving, but if that for your main competitor's product improves more, you will lose share. Unfortunately, most vendors only provide annual benchmark information as a standard offering. If you are in an industry that does not change quickly, that may be reasonable. For most businesses, and to keep customer experience as visible as financial results, you need to report benchmark data quarterly, at the very least.

### The 'Why' matters more than the trends

The score trends for your company and competitors are useless without knowing why. If you buy benchmark reports that do not include reasons why, they are not worthwhile and you should change vendors. The reasons behind positive and negative relative trends need to be explained at the same time as the numbers. The best benchmark vendors also provide improvement suggestions that are customized for your company and your competitors.

### Use rolling quarterly reports for benchmark surveys

It can be expensive to get statistically significant NPS volumes for all of your competitors every quarter. Using a rolling four-quarter average is fine. This means your Q1 report will also include the data from the prior Q2, Q3 and Q4. Drop the oldest quarter as soon as you have a new quarter of data. Your reports should show multiple rolling quarters so trends are easy to understand.

19

# Reliable, trusted metric

The good and bad of double-blind benchmark surveys
The best benchmark surveys are double-blind. This means the people answering the survey do not know who is funding it. Unfortunately, it also means that you have no way of knowing the names of those who have answered. The positive aspect of this is that neither you nor your competitors can try to influence them. On the negative side, you can't follow up with anyone you would like to use as a reference or who has serious concerns.

When you receive benchmark data, it is 'unweighted'. For some businesses, equality of respondents is a good thing. For most businesses equality of all respondents in a bad thing. While you should get data about the sizes of the companies and the job titles of people represented in a business-to-business (B2B) survey panel, I have never seen it used in practice. Customers with large budgets and small budgets are mixed together. Responses from people who are decision-influencers have the same weight as those from decision-makers and indeed from end users. Once you slice and dice the data, you quickly get into issues with the 'law of small numbers'. By this I mean that you will see outliers that are just due to statistical variability in small samples. The subject is tricky, and a later chapter is devoted to it.

I am not aware of any satisfaction benchmark that compares benchmark survey providers. The quality of the benchmark results depends on the relevance of the people who answer the questions. This is probably where you should spend most of your investigation time when selecting a new vendor. Ask to see the profiles of the panel members that will be used for your work. Ask for samples of the text input the vendor has received. They may only be willing to provide it for a different panel, used for a different industry from your own. The vendor should have no difficulty removing company names to make data anonymous.

Panel members usually receive points or other cash-equivalents that they can redeem for merchandise. I don't believe anyone could make a living from being on many panels and taking surveys full-time, though you may have seen get-rich-quick schemes advertised on the internet that suggest it could be done.

# Competitive benchmarks and supplier surveys

Supplier surveys
In business-to-business situations, some customers regularly survey internal users of products and services and provide the resulting feedback to their suppliers. This is a form of benchmark survey in that each supplier is given a report that compares them to other suppliers. In some cases, you will see the names of the comparison companies and other cases they are just shown as 'Company A', 'Company B' and so on. Supplier surveys are my favorite type of B2B research, for a simple reason. Your customer is highly motivated to see you improve.

The first such process I was involved in was Vodafone's Supplier Performance Management initiative. The person who set it up for Vodafone was subsequently headhunted by BP in Houston to do the same. The survey was run by the procurement department. They were measured on supplier performance improvement from year to year. They wanted us to present our improvement initiatives to them, and were very helpful in providing contacts at their end, and helping us with the work. Companies that operate their own supplier surveys usually decline to participate in surveys you may be running.

Correlation and regression analysis can be useful in benchmark studies
If you have limited written commentary and multiple questions have been asked in the benchmark survey, simple correlation analysis can be helpful. Here is a good example from the ICT industry. The Research Board[6] is a Gartner-owned entity. Its members are about 260 CIOs and former CIOs from the Fortune Global 500. One of their annual projects is a supplier survey. Members rate each of their major IT and communications providers on many factors. An anonymized version of one of the results tables is shown in Exhibit 2.1. I used Excel to do simple correlation analysis between the overall scores and individual factors. I then used Excel's conditional formatting to make it more readable. The correlation scores on the right suggest the weight of each question in the overall performance score.

---

[6]  The Gartner CIO Research Board website is at http://www.gartner.com/researchboard/

# Reliable, trusted metric

Correlation, of course, is not the same as causality, and the written comments help. The main body of the table contains the scores, where 5.0 is the maximum possible. Account management comes out as the most important factor. Surprisingly and counter-intuitively, 'understanding of my business' is the least important item. Note in passing that vendor 14 has finished last in the survey for many years and is one of the most profitable companies on the planet. You don't have to be loved to make lots of money. Having an effective monopoly in your area is another way of doing it. The Research Board survey does not include the recommendation question and each company covered only receives customer comments and improvement suggestions for their own company. Since there is no charge to the vendors for the report, it is fabulous value.

## Exhibit 2.1

Example of Research Board results

| | Vendor 1 | Vendor 2 | Vendor 3 | Vendor 4 | ... | Vendor 12 | Vendor 13 | Vendor 14 | |
|---|---|---|---|---|---|---|---|---|---|
| OVERALL PERFORMANCE IN MY ACCOUNT | 4 | 3.9 | 3.8 | 3.8 | ... | 3.1 | 3.1 | 3 | Correlation |
| Understanding of my business | 3.1 | 3.8 | 3.7 | 3.4 | ... | 2.8 | 3.5 | 3.1 | 0.47 |
| Ability to deliver globally | 4.1 | 3.9 | 3.8 | 3.9 | ... | 4.2 | 3.6 | 3.4 | 0.48 |
| Ability to collaborate with other suppliers in my account | 3.5 | 3.7 | 3.7 | 3.7 | ... | 3 | 3.4 | 2.8 | 0.85 |
| Consistent account mgmt across all products and services | 3.7 | 3.9 | 3.5 | 3.7 | ... | 3.3 | 3 | 2.7 | 0.91 |
| Quality and consistency of account teams | 3.6 | 4 | 3.3 | 3.6 | ... | 3.1 | 3.2 | 2.9 | 0.84 |
| Fairness / transparency of pricing, contracts, and licensing | 3.9 | 3.1 | 3.1 | 3.1 | ... | 2.9 | 2.4 | 2.1 | 0.79 |
| Quality of products and services | 4.2 | 3.9 | 4 | 3.9 | ... | 3.8 | 3.4 | 3.5 | 0.79 |
| Vision and ability to innovate | 4.4 | 3.8 | 4 | 3.9 | ... | 4.1 | 3.3 | 3.1 | 0.56 |

## Syndicated benchmark surveys may be the future

When I have shared benchmark survey results with my equivalents at other high-tech companies, I have been pleased to see that the NPS numbers and trends look similar in their surveys. This simply suggests that there are good NPS benchmark vendors covering high-tech. All customer experience leaders I have met have been highly irritated by competitors that publish non-benchmark scores, representing them as fair comparisons. This makes me feel that a good solution for many industries would be for the leading vendors to get together and agree to use a single benchmark provider as their reference. I believe it would be easy to get competitors to agree on the core NPS questions. Each would be free to pay the survey provider for additional questions if they so wished. Additional companies would be free to pay a fee to join the consortium. I suppose a challenge is that non-customer-experience executives from companies that do poorly would want to cut off the vendor, rather than address their issues. Bain and JD Power have recently announced a benchmarking collaboration, and I hope it will go in this direction.

## 2.3 Relationship research

A good relationship feedback process could be described as a non-anonymous mono-vendor benchmark survey. You usually only get detailed information about your own company. If you just have a small number of customers, say less than a hundred, you should simply interview them all face-to-face. If you have a large number of customers, you should segment the customers in some way, using increasing depth for your most important customers. Deeper surveys do not mean asking more questions. The Net Promoter System format remains intact. When you interview your most important customers, you go into far greater depth on the 'Why?' and 'What should we improve?' questions. Clarifying the input right away will make it far easier to prepare a worthwhile improvement plan for the customer to approve.

It is certainly possible to add questions about competitors to your relationship survey, though it would dilute the focus on your own company's improvement opportunities. In cases where your product and your competitor's are mutually exclusive, meaning nobody would buy from both companies, adding questions about competition would give you an early indication about whether customers are thinking of changing. For example, "Why do you buy from us instead of [insert key competitor name]?

### Resellers and other partners
Companies that help you to sell or implement your products and services are a special case. Since their job is to recommend your products and services, asking them the recommendation question is not appropriate. I recommend asking "Please rate your overall satisfaction as an Acme partner", followed by the usual "Why?" and "What should we improve?" Since your partners have the choice of working with other suppliers, they are a good source of competitive information. I therefore suggest adding the

following questions, using a reseller example, and supposing that the main competitors are called Alpha and Beta:

- Do you sell products from Alpha or Beta?
- What can Acme do to make it easier for you to recommend us over Alpha and Beta?

## Future-facing relationship segmentation

I believe it is more useful to segment your research and improvement process by your future revenue expectations for a customer, rather than by what you achieve now. This means that customers who spend a lot on your type of product or service deserve a lot of attention, no matter who they spend it with. I suggest a two-year time horizon. The segmentation is used to determine the type of feedback process you will use. The top tier should be interviewed face-to-face, the second tier by phone or Skype and the lowest tier by email / web. The depth of your loop-closing and improvement commitments will also vary by tier.

## Exhibit 2.2

Using an organization chart to report relationship survey and trends

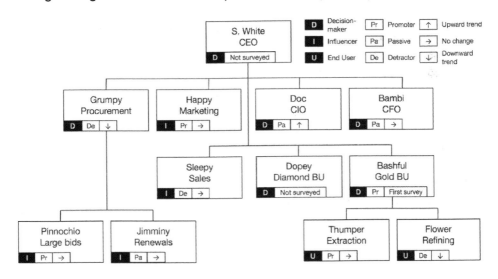

## Reliable, trusted metric

**Publish strategic relationship NPS numbers and trends by individual, not by company**

Account-level NPS metrics can be counter-productive. If you mainly publish relationship NPS scores for each individual customer and perhaps a table that compares the scores, your metric will never be reliable. Account teams who do not look good on the list will do everything possible to manipulate the process so they do better the next time. To ensure reliability, publish the scores and trends by individual person in the customer relationship map. Your overall relationship with a customer is largely the sum of a number of individual relationships. These are what need to be monitored and improved, or referenced. Improvements should be agreed with each person. Even at the level of the individual, the trend is more important than the absolute number. Exhibit 2.2 is a suggestion about how to show the relevant information quite simply.

## 2.4   Product, service and project feedback

Unless your company only sells a single product or service, you need a separate process to gather feedback about each product or service you sell. While benchmark and relationship surveys cover a variety of people and job roles at the customer end, product and service feedback should come from the end users. To get reliable and credible information, you should ask for it when you are explicitly planning to use it. For a service contract that you are going to renegotiate, get feedback from the end users before the negotiation starts and use it to present a more convincing case for renewal.

For products, tell the end users that you are starting a new design cycle, solicit their suggestions, and tell them which suggestions were most common and will be included in the next product or version. If you have customers who are references for your product, pay particular attention to what they say. Your most reliable feedback will come from customers who actively use the product or service. For this type of survey, I don't think it matters whether they have purchased it recently or not. Indeed, an end user may have no idea when the purchase decision was made. If your survey is about something like software that has versions, you will need to ask the users what version they are using if you don't already know. If so, make sure you tell the users how to determine the version number.

Project surveys

Assuming you want to improve the way you plan and deliver customer projects, a formal feedback process is good practice. I have never seen these done well and they are indeed tricky. I believe you should consider project surveys as the least reliable in your portfolio. The reasons are quite complex, and change somewhat between shorter (up to three months) and longer projects:

- The people who will answer the survey are most often chosen when the project is complete (for shorter projects) or when a major

27

milestone has been achieved. Since the project team normally chooses the people who should provide feedback, they have an understandable tendency to select only those who will give favorable answers. Ideally, this can be offset by agreeing the names or job titles of those who will respond in the project contract. Unfortunately, I have never seen this done, both because people want to use standard contracts, and because they do not want to "waste time negotiating details."

- Another possibility is to be clear, both in theory and in practice, that you are not going to measure the project team on the customer feedback. Emphasize that you will use the feedback to improve the processes and tools for all projects, as well as to plan the development of project team members. It is almost impossible to communicate this credibly. Are you really willing to discard customer feedback when putting project team members through their performance reviews? The only thing left is to have a person outside the project team agree the names of those who will provide feedback. This can be the executive sponsor for the customer, if you have one, or the sales leader assigned to the customer.

- For longer projects, the members of the project team and the overall project manager may change over time. It is quite common to see a first team for a proof of concept, a second team for a pilot and a third team for a comprehensive rollout. In such situations, you should not have a single feedback process, but have at least one for each phase. Working purely by phase is deficient too, as lack of project management continuity across phases is a common customer complaint.

- While remaining aware of the aforementioned defects, my recommendation is to track trends by manager of project managers. It seems reasonable to expect that a single project manager will introduce the same conscious or unconscious bias to all project surveys over time. Tracking at the manager level will smooth it out somewhat.

# Product, service and project feedback

## Projects involving Alliances

Most people think of alliances between companies as being two-way affairs. However, it commonly takes three or more companies to implement a customer project, and any research process must take that into account. If a customer receives a survey from only one of the companies involved in implementing a project, they are likely to be surprised. An example may help here.

When I was managing certain software alliances at Compaq, I got a surprise. I had Lotus as one of the services alliances I led at a worldwide level. Lotus had been acquired by IBM about 18 months previously. IBM encouraged them to continue to act as though they were independent. One consequence of this was their love of Compaq. 55% of all the Lotus Notes installations were being sold on Compaq ProLiant servers, and the proportion was increasing slowly, to the irritation of Lotus's new masters. I was in their Cambridge Mass. HQ, trying to work out how to use services to grow our joint business. It turned out that neither Lotus nor Compaq wanted to be 'Prime contractor' for any Notes implementations. A simple two-way alliance was pointless.

Further discussion revealed that the largest Notes implementer on the planet was PricewaterhouseCoopers (PwC), and that this was particularly the case in EMEA. I met repeatedly with the head of the PwC Notes practice in Zurich, and we were successful in some three-way projects with Lotus. (Then HP tried and failed to acquire PwC, ruining the PwC/Compaq work, though this is not directly relevant here.) Two- and three-way alliances are quite common for customer projects. You need to agree a single approach to surveying the whole project and driving improvements together.

## Training surveys

Since I have taken many training courses over the years, I have been surveyed many times. Surveys tend to be quite long and to involve rating the teachers. Oddly, I don't recall ever being asked what any individual teacher could improve. I feel NPS can be used in a hierarchical way, starting with an overall course score, and the usual Why and Improve questions. This can be followed by the same three questions for each teacher. I do not

## Reliable, trusted metric

believe you should ask about the course material, facilities, catering, accommodation and so on. If they matter, they will come up in the written comments. Unfortunately, trainers tend to want to train you on how to answer the surveys. They will typically show a slide that gives a sample score (always a 10), and sample comments, which are always positive. This is a misguided approach and means the trainers do not get many of the improvement suggestions they need.

## 2.5  Microsoft example

Microsoft has an interesting method of getting real-time NPS feedback on their PC/Mac products. They introduced pop-up surveys and the Feedback Hub with the Windows 10 anniversary update. They cover Office 365 as well. Some people around me say they have seen them before Windows 10 came out. In any case, I am impressed.

Pop-up survey

This type of short survey is becoming more common when using applications and websites. Microsoft's version is good in that the entire survey is visible in the pop-up window.

### Exhibit 2.3

Microsoft Windows pop-up survey

Allez-vous recommander Windows 10 à un ami ou un collègue ?

○ 1    ○ 2    ○ 3    ◉ 4    ○ 5

Très improbable                    Très probable

Expliquez pourquoi.

I don't think anyone actually chooses Windows 10 or Mac OS. You choose the applications you want to use and the hardware that seems to be nice-looking. I am happy to recommend my hardware, but not my operating system. It would never occur to me to do so.

☐ You may contact me for more details

By giving us feedback, you agree that Microsoft can use your feedback to improve our products and services. Privacy statement

Submit

It could of course be improved by adding a box to input your improvement suggestions. Exhibit 2.1 is what it looked like when I filled it in. Note that my Windows installation is in French and the pop-up was strangely bilingual. The recommendation question is on a five-point scale. In-application pop-ups tend to have quite high response rates, often above 20%, and occasionally above 30%. I find some supplier claims of "up to 70%" a bit hard to believe. If you are dealing with suppliers who say this, ask whether the Why question is part of the pop-up. If not, their optimistic response rate numbers may only be for the rating, which is far less important than the commentary.

## Exhibit 2.4

Microsoft Feedback Hub

Welcome

Give us feedback to make Windows better

**Send us your feedback to help make Windows better**
Your feedback is essential to helping us make Windows great. Start sharing your feedback by typing in the box at the top of the page or selecting Feedback.

Learn more

**Learn more about Windows and get help**
Make the most out of your Windows experience by visiting the Get Started app. We'll help you set up your device and show you what's new in Windows 10. If you'd like some help with a problem, visit Microsoft Support.

Open the Get Started app
Go to Microsoft Support

**Become a Windows Insider**
Help shape the future of Windows! If you love getting early access to new features and want to help us build Windows, then sign up to become a Windows Insider.

Join the Windows Insider Program

# Microsoft example

Immediate follow-up

Once you have answered the survey, you are taken to the Feedback Hub, which is part of Windows and is shown in Exhibit 2.4. I immediately searched for a variety of minor problems and found useful suggestions for some of them. I liked the ability to 'upvote', meaning to give a higher priority to items of your choice. For one item, 'erratic scrolling', there were quite a lot of different topics, and I suppose Microsoft will have to find a way of automatically grouping the input to make it useful.

## Exhibit 2.5

Office feedback opportunities on a Mac

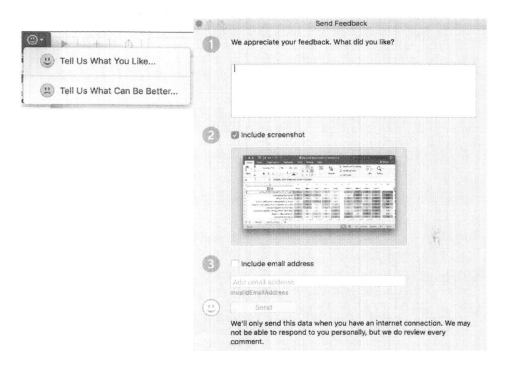

PC and Mac feedback opportunities differ

The Mac versions of Office 365 currently have a feedback option that is not present in the Windows version. See Exhibit 2.5. You can find a small smiley face in the top-right corner of each application. You get an opportunity to provide immediate feedback, though no commitment is made to respond, which is unfortunate.

## Lessons for others

If you don't have the resources to do something quite that sophisticated for your application or web page, you could still send customers directly to an online product discussion forum right after they respond to your survey. It is easy to find voting widgets for WordPress, or you can simply ask people to reply to 'upvote' an improvement suggestion.

# 2.6 Transactional / episode feedback

Transactional surveys are by far the most common type of research. It is helpful to think of them as feedback about 'episodes' or 'jobs to be done'. Customers interact with you to try to accomplish some individual thing as part of their overall experience with you. An overall season of a TV series, for example, consists of a series of episodes. A customer may phone your support center to try to resolve a problem. Resolving the problem is the job they want to get done. Your research should be about that entire job, and not about a sub-component. Customer feedback about the components is only useful in the context of the overall 'job' they need you to do. Transactional / episode research is most appropriate in three situations:

1. Use them to periodically validate that improvements in your customer-centric operational metrics do indeed improve customer satisfaction. For example, your customer complaint handling metrics may show that all complaints are fully resolved within 48 hours. Do your customers agree that this is the case? Perhaps your agents have incentives that push them to close cases that are not actually resolved.

2. Obtaining customer feedback that cannot easily be derived from operational metrics. Let's suppose you have done a metric validation survey and have discovered that there is a disconnect between your operational metrics and what customers think about complaint handling. You know there is a problem, but don't have the information necessary to fix it. What exactly is going on, as perceived by customers? Resist the temptation to ask about the politeness of the person on the phone and a long list of items you might think of. Just use the NPS format and ask the customers why, and what should be improved.

3. As quality indicators for subcontracting agreements. Let's suppose you have contracted with a trucking company to deliver goods, or have contracted with a third party to process your employees' travel

expense claims. You may have specified certain quality or satisfaction levels in the contract, and need to check that the company you are using meets your standards.

You may be surprised that I do not list something like "100% validation that customers are happy with telephone support". You will never get 100% of the customers to answer, and your operational metrics and responses to the scripts you use should tell you this in any case. Over the years, I have seen that many call center scripts do not actually ask customers whether their issue has been resolved. I find this odd and recommend always asking, if you don't already know for certain. If you work in software, please resist the temptation to consider a software defect as resolved if it has been agreed that it will be fixed in the next version. The customer's issue is only resolved when the software has been released and the customer has installed it. You should leave the case open until then, to ensure correct follow up. Customers love to be remembered, and will appreciate the call at the appropriate time.

## NPS may not be the solution for everything

There are types of transactional surveys where I feel NPS is not the best solution. You may still like to use it, simply to avoid having to communicate an additional measurement system within your company. Willingness to recommend a company or product is mainly an overall brand metric. While an individual transaction can destroy your standing with a customer, it is really unlikely that an individual transaction can cause a customer to recommend you all on its own. NPS does not have predictive value for the revenue of telephone support businesses, for example. If you can deal with the communication challenges, you may be better off using Customer Effort Score for many types of transactional surveys. Customer Effort Score measures how hard customers found it to do certain things, like solve a problem. The authors have demonstrated that it predicts revenue for support businesses.

## NPS has additional questions for transactional surveys

In the current version of the Net Promoter System for transactional surveys, the usual Recommendation and Why questions are followed by additional questions: "To what extent has your latest experience made you more or less likely to recommend [company]?" followed by an additional Why question. While this makes the format longer, it provides information on the positive or negative impact individual transactions may have on your overall brand perception.

## Difficulties for service center research
It is challenging to use NPS, or indeed any other research system to gain insights about telephone service centers. The reason is simple. As documented in The Effortless Experience[7] by Dixon, Toman and Delisi, most customers who contact you by phone are simultaneously trying to answer their questions or resolve their issues on your website or elsewhere. It is therefore difficult to know precisely what resolution process their survey responses refer to. The customer could have found 90% of the information they needed from a third-party website, and just received confirmation from you by phone. Think of this as you choose the wording of your questionnaire.

## Pop-ups
Personally, I find pop-up web surveys for transactions irritating. I suppose they must work for some companies, or we would not see them anymore. Best practice is to have at least the rating scale directly in the pop-up, like the Windows 10 pop-up already discussed. If you are not able to work out how to capture text feedback within the pop-up, clicking on one of the numbers should take you to a web page to answer the remaining questions.

## Conclusion
Transactional surveys are over-used in my opinion. Customers are almost never informed about what you have learned or what you are doing with the results. Indeed, even where I have been responsible for the implementation of transactional surveys, I never included a process for summarizing what we had learned and informing customers, so shame on me too. In most cases, the surveys are used to generate metrics, not action. Surveys are

---

[7] Matthew Dixon, Nick Toman and Rick Delisii: *The Effortless Experience*, Portfolio, ISBN1591845815

sometimes implemented when neither people nor funding are available to work on the improvements that might be required. Yes, there may well be a 'Hawthorne effect'[8], in that many studies have shown that the simple fact of demonstrating you are paying attention to something does indeed improve its performance. I liken that to the placebo effect of 'alternative' medicines. These effects are worthwhile, but are not a great substitute for intervening and fixing what ails you.

---

[8] The psychological experiments at the GE Hawthorne plant are described in the Wikipedia article at https://en.wikipedia.org/wiki/Hawthorne_effect

## 2.7   What is a good score?

"OK, I have my NPS number. Is it good or bad?" There are two parts to the answer. First, the score does not tell you much on its own. The reasons customers give for the scores and what they want you to improve are more important. Second, the absolute number is meaningless. What matters are how it compares to your competition and whether it is improving or getting worse. Let's start by talking about the score.

### Scores vary greatly by industry

Not alone are average NPS scores quite different by industry, they vary widely within an industry. Exhibit 2.6 shows the results of a Temkin benchmark survey, for example. The overall message you should take here is that a single number is meaningless in isolation. An NPS of 15 is horrible for a supermarket and approaches best-in-class for an ISP or cable TV provider. There is one subtlety in NPS theory that is worth noting here: you gain or lose share when your NPS trend is more or less favorable compared to the leading competitor. The Temkin table considers all competitors to be equal when calculating the average score. Some of the extreme scores below will be for companies that may not be relevant (unless they happen to be your own company).

Moving from the facts in the chart to personal opinion, the five industries at the bottom of the table seem to share some characteristics. They are mainly companies that either are monopolies or used to be monopolies. In many cities or neighborhoods, there used to be only one way of getting TV, which was via your local cable network provider. Internet Service Providers suffered from a similar lack of competition. It is somewhat unfortunate that the new alternatives to cable television are dependent on ISPs for delivery.

As noted at the bottom, the graph expresses the views of US consumers. I believe the relative positions of different industries do not change much by country. The scores do vary by country, as will be discussed later.

## Exhibit 2.6

Temkin NPS benchmarks for various industries

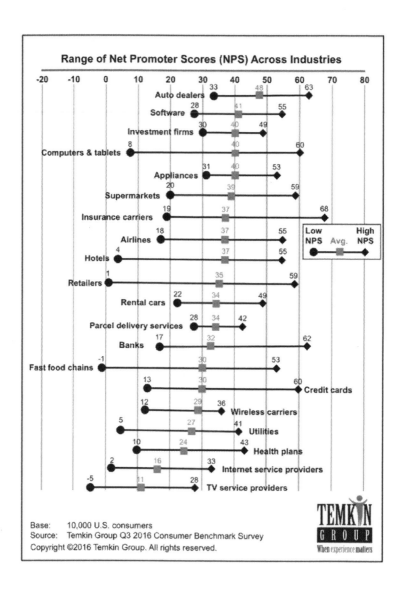

# What is a good score?

## Validation using CSAT scores by industry

The variations by industry are of course not unique to NPS. Exhibit 2.7 shows the American Customer Satisfaction Index scores by industry as of late 2016. The pattern resembles that for NPS scores. Since NPS numbers can vary from -100 to +100, and ACSI numbers only from 0 to 100, it is normal that there is far less variation in the ACSI scale. Remember that these are not NPS numbers.

## Exhibit 2.7

ACSI scores by industry sector

| Industry sector | 2015 | 2016 | % Change |
|-----------------|------|------|----------|
| Energy utilities | 74.3 | 71.9 | -3.2% |
| Health care & social assistance | 75.1 | 76.1 | 1.3% |
| Transportation | 73.1 | 75.0 | 2.6% |
| Telecommunications and information | 68.8 | 70.1 | 1.9% |
| Accommodation and food services | 78.3 | 78.7 | 0.5% |
| Manufacturing / durable goods | 78.8 | 81.9 | 3.9% |
| Manufacturing / nondurable goods | 76.7 | 82.1 | 7.0% |
| Finance & insurance | 74.8 | 76.5 | 2.3% |
| Retail trade | 74.8 | 78.3 | 4.7% |
| Public administration / government | 63.9 | 70.3 | 10.0% |
| E-commerce | 79.5 | 82.4 | 3.6% |
| E-business | 74.4 | 74.9 | 0.7% |

## Communicating the 'goodness' of your NPS scores

Once you are confident you understand the range of scores for your industry and geographical coverage, I suggest communicating some round numbers in a consistent way. For example, if you are in the supermarket business in the USA, try saying "30 is good, 40 is great, 50 is world-class." Make sure you understand where your most important competitor is within the range.

## Reliable, trusted metric

Recognizing 'marketing' NPS scores

I suppose I am being polite here. I have seen too many companies trumpeting things like "Our NPS is 92." Without any qualifier, the only acceptable source you should use for such statements is a reputable double-blind benchmark survey. If you use anything else, you should at least provide the source. I have been reading double-blind benchmark survey results for many industries for many years. I have never seen a score of 92. More on this later.

# 2.8   How to use verbatim answers

While our rational minds like to see scores and trends, the primary value of Net Promoter System surveys lies in the answers to the "Why?" and "What should we improve?" questions. Interpreting and using these answers well is quite challenging. Indeed, it is so challenging that many companies don't really try. Communicating trends in numbers is far easier than finding and communicating trends in text. Avoiding our personal biases when looking at the answers is tricky too. We will cover software solutions for text analysis in the section on infrastructure. Here are some considerations on other points.

## The answers do not change quickly

Once you have been gathering feedback for some time, you will see that the most common answers to the verbatim questions change more slowly than NPS scores. This makes it difficult to maintain management interest. The main way to make people want to listen is to focus on personalization. By this I mean using quotes from specific named customers as examples of each response theme you are presenting. I suppose you can think of it as though you were directing a reality TV show. The most extreme comments are the ones that will attract the most attention. Of course, many comments will be entertaining, but not actually useful. Care is needed to ensure they support the improvement initiatives you are proposing.

## Some answers matter more than others

You will quickly learn that some things are only mentioned by Detractors, and others only by Promoters. Understanding which are which is critical to understanding the items that are hygiene factors, meaning they just need to be 'good enough'. Psychologist Frederick Herzberg developed his two-factor theory of motivation. At its core, 'motivators' can only motivate people, and 'hygiene factors' can only demotivate them. Once hygiene factors are good enough, nobody cares about them. When communicating them, I suggest separating the groupings, presenting just one at a time.

- 'Just not good enough' is the set of three to five things that Detractors most often give as reasons for being detractors. If Passives and Promoters don't mention them in their answers to the "Why" question, they are clearly hygiene factors. Once you improve them to the point where they are good enough, you don't need to spend any more.
- 'Potential loyalty drivers'' are the most common improvement suggestions made by Promoters that do not come up as much from the other categories.
- 'Communication opportunities' are things that commonly come up as improvement suggestions, but which you have already implemented. To pick an example, this might be a suggestion for a feature that is already in your software program, but is not as easy to find as it might be, or may be missing from your manual or help file.

## Competitive comparisons are the key

The key to competitive advantage lies of course in the comparison between what customers say about you and what they say about your competitors. Using hygiene factors as an example, competitive comparisons are the only way you can know whether something some customers complain about is 'good enough' or not. A hygiene factor is 'good enough' if customers don't complain about you more than they do about your competitors.

Beyond hygiene factors, if the most common improvement suggestion for the leading competitor's product is something your product already does, this fact needs to be in your sales people's 'battle cards' for competitive bids, or clearly communicated as such to your resellers. Maintain interest by showing trends over time.

If, for example, you can see that comments on a competitor's product quality have been improving markedly, while yours have been getting worse, that should grab your audience's attention. Support the relative trend discussion by including direct customer quotes.

# How to use verbatim answers

## The difference between the Why and Improve responses

When a customer is angry with you, the Why and Improve responses are often about the same problem. "I had to wait 20 minutes in the checkout queue" is often followed by a suggestion to "Hire more people to shorten queues at peak times." So, for Detractors, asking both questions can seem superfluous. This is not the case for Promoters. For the same store as the Detractor, a Promoter might give "Great variety of modern furniture that suits my budget" as the reason they like you, and still say "Hire more people to shorten checkout queues" as an improvement suggestion.

## Using people to study text responses

If you decide not to use software to study verbatim responses, ask a variety of people to study the data and propose the top three themes in each category. This is a type of work where using an 'outsider' is counter-productive. Everyone you ask to help must understand the subject matter in some detail. You are looking for expert views. If you have responses in languages your experts do not speak, using Google or Microsoft's automatic translation software works well enough, and is of course far better than discarding those answers.

# 2.9 Avoiding confirmation bias when interpreting results

In his book *Thinking, Fast and Slow*[9], Daniel Kahneman describes two ways our brains function. He refers to them as 'System 1' and 'System 2'. At their most superficial, you can think of System 1 as intuition, and System 2 as rational thought. He offers persuasive arguments that System 1 acts first, and that System 2 is lazy, and does its best to avoid work.

Relevance to NPS

For NPS to be a trusted metric, it must work for both System 1 and System 2. The Ultimate Question 2.0 concentrates on System 2. This book's content on survey design, improving response rates and things like the automated analysis of verbatim responses all appeal to System 2. I consider the System 2 work to be necessary but insufficient for success. You also have to appeal to the fast-acting intuitive reactions of System 1 thinking. The following are some items for you to consider.

Sequence of presentation

Kahneman describes an experiment set up by Solomon Asch[10]: subjects were given descriptions of two people and asked for comments on their personalities. Here they are. What do you think of Alan and Ben?

• Alan: intelligent, industrious, impulsive, critical, stubborn, envious.
• Ben: envious, stubborn, critical, impulsive, industrious, intelligent.

Most people describe Alan far more positively than Ben. Because the first word used to describe Alan is 'intelligent', the more negative character traits

---

[9] Daniel Kahneman: Thinking, Fast and Slow, published by Farrar, Straus and Giroux, 2011, ISBN 978-037427631

[10] The full set of Asch's experiments in this area is described in the article below. The example used is "Experiment VI" in the article.
http://www.all-about-psychology.com/solomon-asch.html

are considered to be justified. However, the words used to describe Alan and Ben are identical. Only the sequence has changed. The first thing that is presented has a disproportionate effect on your message, and sets the tone for all the rest. For example, if the overall message you want to communicate is that your company is making good progress, don't start with the only negative story. When you are going to talk about what you need to improve and what is going well, start with what is going well. Of course, if you have just taken over the customer experience responsibility, you may want to be Machiavellian and start with the bad news, implicitly blaming it on the prior leadership. You could then reverse the sequence for the same information a few weeks later, and people will think you are making progress. Naturally, if you do this blatantly or often, you will lose trust.

## Jumping to conclusions

We all jump to conclusions without being aware of it. Kahneman offers the example, "Ann approached the bank" to illustrate this point. You almost certainly formed an image of a woman walking towards a bank, possibly to deposit money. However, the statement is ambiguous. If we had also been told that Ann was on a canoeing trip, our conclusion would be different and we would see her paddling to the side of the river.

A lot of customer experience information is ambiguous. People's System 1 will jump to conclusions and System 2 will sleep, unless you force it into action. You have probably heard of the metaphor of blind people trying to identify what they are touching, when each is able to feel just one part of an elephant. Turn this on its head and you have confirmation bias. If your audience has been primed to think, for example, that customer service is awful, they will use whatever they can in your data to support that conclusion, and may not even realize they are doing so.

How to get System 2 to work

In other words, how do you get people to react totally rationally to the NPS numbers you present and the financial business case you may be making? The sad truth is that you can't do much about it. Your best solution is to force your System 1 to look at what you are going to present. Think in terms of someone who is going to ignore most of the data. What are they going to see when they look at your slides? What are they going to hear when you speak? Their intuitive, emotional reaction will win out. System 2 will act only for brief periods. Plan on it.

There is some science that suggests that asking people to do a simple mathematical puzzle that requires System 2 to get the correct answer will help engage System 2, at least for a brief period. Priming people by giving them a puzzle to do in a break, or just having it on the screen before your presentation may help. There is also evidence that making something difficult to read forces System 2 to engage. In any case, you should kick off by using a real customer quote or example, appealing to your audience's emotions before you start showing data.

# 2.10 The law of small numbers

Continuing the discussion on System 1 versus System 2, some curious things happen when people study surprising data.

### Kidney cancer in the United States

Daniel Kahneman asked his readers to consider the example of the data for the incidence of kidney cancer in the 3,141 counties of the United States. "The counties in which the incidence of kidney cancer is lowest are mostly rural, sparsely populated, and located in traditional Republican states in the Midwest, the South and the West. What do you make of this?" I have recently seen a similar type of study here in Switzerland. Our rational minds immediately get busy trying to analyze why the geography or being Republican might cause cancer. For the Swiss study, I worked out that it was probably the healthy rural lifestyles that provided the benefit. Fresh air, fresh vegetables, plenty of exercise. How could that not be the reason?

### What about the worst places?

However, the counties with the highest incidence of kidney cancer had exactly the same profile. The somewhat similar Swiss study concentrated on this aspect. The TV news report interviewed a person who talked about the use of pesticides in agriculture, various treatments in the vineyards and so on. Seems perfectly logical to think that the rural population would be far more exposed to them. In addition, the rural populations are poorer and probably have more difficulty getting high-quality health care. There were discussions of 'cancer clusters' in areas with the highest rates.

### The key word was…

In reality, the most important words in the description of the counties with high rates of kidney cancer were 'sparsely populated'. Counties in the United States have populations that range from under 500 to over 10 million. According to www.kidneycancer.org, the lifetime likelihood of anyone contracting kidney cancer is 1 in 63. In a small county, it does not take many cases for the percentage to be unusually high. The general randomness of cancer over the entire country means that there will of course be some small counties, with quite small numbers of cancers, but with relatively high or relatively low incidence percentages. The extremes are what grab the headlines. Next time you see a story about something like scientists studying why people in some small village live such long lives, treat it with suspicion. A similar village just down the road may have a population with an unusually short average lifespan. That's statistics!

## Use care when presenting your data

Customer experience data commonly has small numbers. If, for example, you are presenting NPS scores for 40 countries, it is very likely that both the highest and lowest scores will be from countries with relatively small sample sizes. This has little to do with statistical significance. If you are looking at enough items, each with 90% confidence, one in ten is just going to be a relatively poor reflection of reality. I used to present NPS benchmark scores for 45 enterprise software companies each quarter. It was very common to see a new small company top the list for a single quarter. If trends from prior quarters did not support this, I told my audience we should wait until the following quarter to react. If the prior quarterly trends did support it (as was the case with ServiceNow's gradual move from awful NPS scores to great ones), I proposed immediate action.

## Nobel laureates by per capita

Another entertaining example and research question would be the following: Why do the Faroe Islands have the highest number of Nobel Prizes by capita? Let's send out a research team to study their education system and copy it everywhere! In fact, the reason is that they have had one Nobel, and have a population of just over 48,000.

## Regression to the mean

If you have loads of data and a consistent trend for something, such as transactional NPS scores for a call center, be careful how you react when you see a substantial short-term change from the trend. To give an analogy, behavioral psychologists generally agree that punishing children for unusually bad behavior does not work, and can even have negative long-term effects. (These psychologists believe that rewarding good behavior works far better.) However, most parents believe punishment does work, and works well. The reason for this belief is regression to the mean. The child has a certain average behavior, trending in a certain direction. They then do something that is unacceptable, and outside the prior average. The parent punishes them and the behavior returns to the prior average. That would have happened in any case, even without any intervention. That is, it will regress to the mean. The only time you have act in new ways is when the trend has actually changed (as it does in fact do if you reward good behavior over time). If you are constantly seen to reward or punish people for what are really single random deviations from their normal trend, you will lose credibility.

# 2.11 Should I adjust my data before reporting?

Suppose you have performed an NPS survey and feel the data set is not representative of your customers. What should you do?

A common issue, rarely addressed
Throughout my customer experience career, I have never adjusted my data sets before or after analyzing them. This has always made me somewhat uncomfortable. Think about these examples:

- Your competitive benchmark survey provider uses a panel of people in countries around the world. You do 60% of your business in the USA, 15% in Canada, 10% in the UK, and smaller percentages in over thirty countries. The survey provider panel is 40% in the USA, 10% in Canada, 15% in the UK, 10% each in France, Germany and Australia, and 5% in another twenty countries. Should you take the survey provider data and re-weight it to reflect the profile of your company? At HP, we did not have any data for Japan the year of the earthquake and tsunami. That had a material impact on the worldwide averages, but we did not call it out in the reports. Was this some subconscious decision because the missing Japanese data made the overall results slightly better?
- You run project completion surveys for your consulting company. Customers pay vastly different prices for different types of projects, varying by a factor of 100:1. Should you weight the survey responses by revenue, giving 100 times the weight to a response for an expensive project?
- Your relationship survey covers two CxOs, three other decision-makers, five decision-influencers and ten end users. Should you weight the survey so the responses from CxOs count more?
- You run transactional surveys after calls are closed in your service center. You code calls by their level of severity, into critical, high, medium and low. Should critical calls have more weight in your

survey? If 10% of your calls are in the critical category, but only 5% of your survey responses, should you double the weight of those survey responses?

## No consensus, major consequences

There is no consensus on the topic. The reason is that it is difficult to take an unbiased decision when adjusting data sets. This is of course not just the case for customer experience data. The New York Times published an article on the subject in September 2016, while the Trump-Clinton contest was in its final stages. The Upshot[11] gave 867 voter intention responses to four different highly respected pollsters, and studied the data themselves. Each person or team studying the data adjusted it using their own methodology. Adjustments were made to reflect race, gender and age to reflect the population of Florida, source of the data. Further adjustments were made to reflect likely voting intention. For example, if Hispanics are less likely to vote than Whites, some adjusted the poll results to reflect it. Others considered whether the people polled said they had voted in prior elections. The variations in methodology produced a greater variation in results than would be expected only from sampling error. The difference in views varied by five points. One showed Trump winning by one point; another showed Clinton winning by three points. History tells us that Clinton won the popular vote by two points.

## Conclusion

I am not against adjusting an analysis to force data to better match your customer profile. I am against doing such adjustments differently each time, or having different principles for different types of surveys. Either you adjust to reflect customer revenue profiles, geography and other factors, or you don't. You need to be consistent. If you have multiple businesses in your company, the same principles should be used by all, all the time. If you use a benchmark survey provider that customizes a solution specifically for you, you should agree response quotas in your most important customer

---

[11]   The New York Times article on how polls are adjusted before publication is here: http://www.nytimes.com/interactive/2016/09/20/upshot/the-error-the-polling-world-rarely-talks-about.html.

dimensions. Do it once, then avoid the temptation to change it for a reasonable period, say three years or so.

## 2.12 Learning check

Decide whether the following statements are true or false. Answers at the back of the book.

1.  If your competitive benchmark NPS number is better than that of your main competitor, you will take market share from them moving forward.
2.  Good NPS scores start at 30, great scores at 40, and you are world-class at 50.
3.  Consistent trends in numbers that are based on small sample sizes are always useful. You do not need sample sizes for all competitors to be the same, for example.
4.  All customers are considered equal by benchmark survey suppliers, so customers who spend a lot have the same weight as those who do not spend much.

# 3. Reliable Trusted Metric - Part 2: Survey design

## 3.1   Deciding whether and when to survey

That crucial moment when survey design died,
and survey dramatic interpretation was born

The first step in designing surveys is being selective about what research you are going to do. Make sure you are going to provide customers with more value than you will extract from them.

Sanity check on whether you should gather feedback at all
Here are some considerations that should help you decide where to start:

1.   Are you going to use any new input you get? If you have already established your top five improvement priorities, have staffed them, are implementing, and can't add a new project in the next six months,

don't do any surveys other than those that provide progress feedback on your improvement work.

2. Taking a software example, if you are planning a new major release and want user input on what should be in it, ask them in a formal way. After 30 years in and out of the software business, as a leader and as a user, I have never once been asked for formal input about what should be in the next version. Product managers generally feel they know what users want, based on informal and anecdotal conversations, rather than research. This of course applies beyond software.

3. Not every customer touchpoint is important. Use your overall brand or benchmark surveys to establish which touchpoints customers mention as competitive advantages or disadvantages, and don't survey anyone about any of the others. To pick a B2B example, surveying people about the friendliness, competence and efficiency of the person who handles a query about the accuracy of an invoice is certain to be a waste of resources that could better be spent elsewhere.

## Timing is everything

Survey timing is an important part of research reliability. Seeking feedback about things that are in the distant past is unlikely to be of much value for example. Here are some appropriate times to consider collecting customer input, by type of survey. What follows presupposes that you are going to use the feedback to make improvements for your customers. If not, there is no good timing.

## Product surveys part 1 - Unboxing and installing your product

Here we are talking about an individual product, not a generic purchase or other touchpoint experience that applies to all your products. Some products are sophisticated (the marketing word for complex) to install. Others are not. If your product takes time and effort to unbox or download, install and use for the first time, it is worthwhile understanding what your customers think of the experience and how it can be improved. The research needs to be done immediately after the experience. Waiting a week or more will mean losing the positive and negative emotional impact.

# Deciding whether and when to survey

If yours is a technology product, I suggest sending the survey request or phoning the customer within 48 hours of delivery. While this will be easy to do in a direct business that sells to consumers, it is more difficult in other circumstances. You want to survey the end user of the product, and they may not be the buyer in a B2B situation, so you might not know who to contact.

If you use resellers, they may not want to provide the customer data, and you should offer to run the survey on their behalf, providing them the data for initial screening. If yours is a software product, the installation routine itself should generate the survey request 24 hours after the installation takes place. Requiring or at least suggesting product registration on a website will give you additional sources of end-user contact details.

## Product surveys part 2 - Usage

In most situations, you won't hear anything from a customer who does not have any problems. Unfortunately, the reason for not having problems could be that the customer no longer uses your product. Perhaps they never started using it in the first place. You need to understand the views of customers who have been using your product for some time, and I suggest six months after purchase as a reasonable target for your research. The purpose, as explained to the customer, should be to get feedback for improving the product itself, as well as future products. In my own experience of software product usage surveys, it is common to get suggestions for additional features that the product already has, but the customer has not been able to find. Usage surveys have the same challenge as installation surveys, meaning you may not know whom to contact.

SaaS (Cloud) software is a completely different in that you do know who is using your software and indeed how much they use it. If a customer who has been using your software suddenly stops, contact them immediately. SaaS software usually allows you to see what functions a customer uses. If you can see that they are not using something they really should be using, you can send them a link to a training video, or send over someone who can talk them through it.

# Survey design

## Service contracts

The ideal time to get feedback on a service contract is a little before the customer is considering renewing it. This is a bit more subtle than it might seem. If you have a large multi-year contract (for example to provide security services to a company) your competitors will probably know about it, and will start to contact your customer well before the contract renewal data. Since your competitors will be saying how wonderful they are, and how awful you are, you need to have acted well before this point. I suggest an annual survey as a minimum for multi-year contracts, taking place half way through each year. If you have a single-year contract, I suggest doing the research about three months in, so that all improvement suggestions can be implemented before the contract comes up for renewal consideration, probably about nine months in.

## Hybrid product / service

An airline flight is a hybrid product & service. This sort of offer should be researched within 24 hours of completion. Most airlines seem to miss the point. Some give you the survey while you are still in the air, not knowing essential things like whether your luggage will show up on the carousel. Others send you the survey after a week or two. Frequent fliers will have completely forgotten about the experience by then, or will confuse it with another flight. This happened to me regularly, as I have been taking over 100 flights per year for nearly as long as I can remember. What did I think of my flight from Atlanta to Paris two weeks ago? Who knows? Since product and service surveys are not mentioned in *The Ultimate Question 2.0*, this may be a good time to reinforce the definition. An entire flight experience, from awareness, to reservation, to the actual trip itself, involves a sequence of touchpoints. Each touchpoint could be studied by a transactional survey. The airline offers many different products and services, the sum of which might be studied in their brand survey.

## Relationship surveys and Brand surveys

Twice a year is a good frequency for your most important customer relationships and may work best for your brand surveys. You may like to run them both on a continuous basis so you can see the effects of things like changes in the economy and your financial and product announcements.

This would mean, for example, sampling one sixth of your customers every month. Remember that you need to report results and improvement projects to customers as well as to your own team.

## Transactional surveys

While it might seem obvious that they should happen shortly after the transaction takes place, it is surprising how rarely this happens. All too often, I get pop-up windows when I have just started an online transaction. I dismiss the window, and then don't think about it anymore. For the simplest transactions, surveying just after they are complete seems appropriate. For more complex things, like telephone support for a technology product, it seems appropriate to wait for 24 hours, as it may take a little time for the customer to know whether the issue has been completely resolved.

## 3.2   Response rates and statistical significance

All survey types are sensitive to response rates. The lower your response rate, the less accurate your survey. Bain analysis shows that surveys with low response rates give over-optimistic results, as the people who like you tend to respond more easily than those who do not. Getting high response rates is primarily a function of the nature of the relationship you have with the people you are surveying. If you are using email to try to survey people you have never met, and with whom you have never done business, you should expect a response rate of 3% or less. At the other extreme, if you have a practice of formally interviewing ten executives from your largest client face-to-face every six months, have been doing so for the last five years, demonstrating that you provide the improvements they request, a 100% response rate is a reasonable expectation.

### Perverse effect of high response rates

High response rates drive lower scores on a constant scale. In my experience with HP, this meant that our deep face-to-face relationship surveys with 80%+ response rates usually produced Net Promoter Scores that were considerably lower than the scores we saw in benchmark surveys or indeed in any other type of survey. Avoid the temptation to compare scores from different types of survey, or at least from surveys with very different response rates.

### Here is what Reichheld and Markey say

My own experience is not an isolated case and others have found similar trends. Based on their many years of experience, Fred and Rob provide some numbers, and I believe the numbers should surprise most people. They show a far greater impact of low response rates than expected. I don't believe the phenomenon is specific to NPS. The principles should apply to all rating systems. Let's suppose you have carried out a survey and the results are as shown in Exhibit 3.1.

# Response rates and statistical significance

## Exhibit 3.1

What about the people who do not participate in the survey?

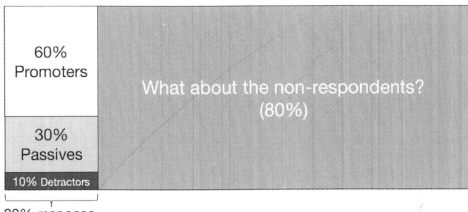

20% response
rate, NPS: 50

The question is, what do the people on the right think? Exhibit 3.2 is what is shown in *The Ultimate Question 2.0*. It represents what would have happened had 100% of the recipients responded to your survey.

## Exhibit 3.2

Effect of answers from the remaining 80%

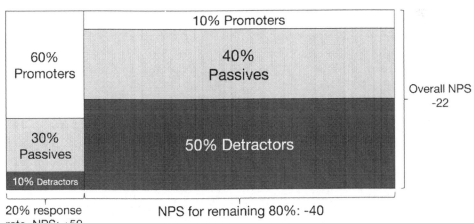

20% response          NPS for remaining 80%: -40
rate, NPS: +50

# Survey design

The theory is that Promoters are the ones most likely to answer your surveys. They like you and want to help. Passives and Detractors are more likely to think you have already wasted enough of their time. Extreme Detractors will still tend to answer.

## Surprise!
This surprises most people. It is a very difficult subject to study as you can't simultaneously get different response rates for the same survey and same audience. What I have seen is that the results from people who take the survey when they receive a follow-up email tend to be lower than for the initial respondents, though I have also seen exceptions. My brother (and this book's illustrator) has a doctorate in Cognitive Psychology and has not been able to design an experiment that would prove the theory. Nonetheless, the psychology suggested by Fred and Rob makes sense to me. (Feel free to accuse me of cognitive bias!)

## Statistical significance
Analysis and determination of statistical significance of results can be challenging. The following statement may seem counter-intuitive: If you want people to trust your metrics, don't include any information about statistical significance in your main communication vehicles. There are two main reasons for this:

- There is no single way to explain significance across all feedback systems. Correctly explaining the significance for each type of survey is long and complex and will make people believe you are manipulating the numbers.
- There are survey types where intuitive significance rules do not apply. For example, if you have 20 customers that represent 60% of your revenue and you have high-quality relationship survey results from 15 of them, you are in great shape. If you try to explain the statistical significance range correctly, some amateur statistician in your audience is bound to say, "There are less than 30 companies in your sample so it can't possibly be significant." If you don't mention significance, there will be fewer opportunities for such people to

embarrass themselves. If the question is asked, well, good luck, and be diplomatic.

Improving response rates
Next, let's look at the key techniques for improving response rates:

- Application of classical direct marketing practices.
- Use of technology when email is used to send survey invitations.
- Work on the quality of your contact list.

# 3.3  Apply direct marketing techniques

Like most people, I receive lots of survey requests by email. Unlike most people, I don't just delete them all. I want to learn. What I usually learn is that most survey designers don't understand even the most basic direct marketing techniques.

### Direct marketing reference source
My direct marketing guru is Drayton Bird, author of *Commonsense Direct & Digital Marketing*[12]. Most of the techniques for getting people to do what you want them to do have not changed since direct marketing was done by sending people things by snail mail. Here are the most critical points:

### Personalize
Make your invitation as personal as conceivably possible. Use the person's first and last name. (It is better to err on the side of formality. There are cultures where using an adult person's first name only will turn them off. France is a good example.) If you have additional information about them, like the city where they live, the industry in which they work and so on, use that too. Personalization applies at the outbound source as well. If you are doing an overall brand image/relationship survey that is being sent by email to smaller customers and partners, it should go out from the CEO's mailbox. Product-specific surveys should go out from the product manager's mailbox and should start with "Good morning Mr. Doe, I am the product manager for the DoubleBubble Jacuzzi you bought recently at Home Depot…"

### Single action request
Only ask the person to take a single action. When I was taught direct marketing, I was taught to think of the recipient holding a stack of letters and standing over a waste bin. The first letter asks the person to do A. She

---

[12]  Drayton Bird: Commonsense Direct & Digital Marketing, Kogan Page, 2007 ISBN 978-0749447601

puts it in an action stack on her desk. The second one asks her to do B. She puts it in the bin. The third one asks her to do A or B… She thinks "Wow, A or B, which should I do? I can't decide." So she drops it in the bin. Like most aspects of direct marketing, this has been studied using A / B testing; the technique where you change only one thing in a marketing piece and measure what happens. While intuition would tell you that giving a person two choices would double the overall response rate, the opposite actually happens. Your overall response rate halves if you give a person two choices rather than asking them to do a single thing. If you give them three choices, response rates drop to a quarter.

## Herd instinct

Appeal to herd instinct. The UK government has a partially privatized unit called the 'Behavioural Insights Team'[13], generally known as the 'Nudge unit'. They have convincingly shown that writing to people who are late paying their taxes in a particular way works. Something like, "Almost every company here in the greater Homeville area has paid their taxes on time. In the last year, these taxes have paid for a new playground on Middle St. and the new recycling centre behind the farmers' market. Please join your fellow citizens in making Homeville a better place to live." Of course, all that has to be true.

Since you are unlikely to get half the recipients of an email to respond to a survey, the reminder could say something like, "Acme customers from all over the greater Chicago area have already answered our three-minute survey and are helping us to improve our lawnmowers. Please add your views to theirs to ensure all of Chicago is represented." Naturally, this requires knowing that that the person does indeed live in that area. Again, the more personal you can make it, the better.

---

[13] Wikipedia article on the Behavioural Insights Team:
https://en.wikipedia.org/wiki/Behavioural_Insights_Team#Using_social_norms_to_incre
ase_tax_payments

# Survey design

## The correct choice of fonts

For some reason, this one is controversial and when I talk about it, I am usually told I am wrong, at least by the people who are being polite. The others use stronger words. The font you use makes a big difference to response rates. You should always use a serif font for body text in your emails or paper forms. Serif fonts are the ones with little hooks on them and with bases on all the vertical strokes. These extra hooks and bases are the serifs. There is a reason 99.999% of all books are written with serif fonts. These fonts are much easier to read.

Most people will recognize Arial as a 'sans-serif' font and Times New Roman as a serif font. The serifs give the eye a natural line to follow. Comprehension is much better than with sans-serif fonts because your eye never accidentally skips to the previous or following line. This is not an issue with short headings. Look around you and you will see that most books and magazines have sans-serif fonts for the short headings, and serif fonts for body text. This has been tested repeatedly in direct marketing, especially by Drayton Bird. The common view that this is no longer the case because so many sans-serif fonts are used on web pages is simply wrong.

## Place pictures carefully, if at all

Don't break up your text with pictures. Drayton Bird's research shows that a high proportion of people won't read anything below your picture. If you have to have a picture, it should be at the top or bottom, or perhaps to one side. Note that if you are sending emails to a new distribution list, the customers' email clients may block the display of images.

Exhibit 3.3 is an example of a survey request I received from Thai Airways. My PC Outlook client blocked the images, though not the button image, while my iPad mail client displayed it correctly. I can't resist noting that while they know that I took the flight, they don't know my name. Did you know that airlines slang for passengers is 'Self-loading freight'? I should be consoled by the fact that they don't know the name of the EVP who sent the email either? I suppose I should complete my pickiness by adding that you should spell out dates to avoid confusion. Thai has used the US date format for a European customer.

## Exhibit 3.3
### Thai Airways survey display problems

Dear Valued Customer,

Thank you for flying THAI.

In order to provide the highest standard of quality service, we would be grateful if you could spare a few minutes to participate the survey related to your travel experience with THAI on *11/02/2016 TG461 BKK - MEL* on *Business Class*. The survey takes a few minutes to complete on-line and it will be expired within 10 days.

**Begin Survey**

Your recommendations will be most valuable to THAI in meeting higher level of customer satisfaction in order to achieve services excellence in accordance with the Company's Core Competency of "World Class, High Trust and Thai Touch".

*For further comment or suggestion, please send e-mail directly to customer@thaiairways.com*

Yours sincerely,

Executive Vice President, Commercial Department
Thai Airways International Public Company Limited

Please do not forward this email as its survey link is unique to you.
Opt out of receiving surveys from this sender

## Reminders

Send a reminder after two days. When you send a survey invitation by email, you will typically get 90% of the responses within 24 hours. Almost nobody files this sort of thing away for later consideration. They either handle it when they see it, or not at all. Only send the reminder to people who have not already responded. If 100 people responded to the first email, about 65 will answer a second email telling them there are only 24 hours left to provide input.

# Survey design

## Incentives

I suppose I should add a word about incentives. Incentives can improve response rates, but should not be used. Way back in early 1994, I ran a project to launch a Digital-Microsoft software subscription service across Europe. It was a precursor to Microsoft's launch of a volume licensing program. The main technique used was direct-response advertising. One country project leader (OK, it was Norway) ignored my advice and included an incentive. The incentive was to be entered in a draw for two tickets to the soccer World Cup in the USA that year. Norway had qualified, to their surprise, and the promotion was a spectacular success. Surprisingly, it almost got me fired. A certain Steve Ballmer was leading sales at Microsoft at the time, and he apparently became irate that we had taken 20% market share in Norway with the promotion. The incumbent Microsoft resellers were unhappy and complained bitterly. My boss's boss's boss (John Rando at the time) had signed the agreement with Microsoft, came to see me, determined that everything was OK and defended me. Whew! In any case, it proved that incentives work, and have consequences.

## Incentives produce positive bias

While that is an extreme case of an incentive, there is a more general issue that has to do with human nature. Providing incentives seems to positively bias responses to surveys. Humans have difficulty believing they can win something in a random prize draw if they give very negative feedback. So, if your intent is just to improve the metrics but not to gain accurate insights, go ahead and use incentives.

## A/B testing

Direct marketing introduced the concept of A/B testing. This is where you change just one thing in an email (for example) and compare the results randomly with emails that do not have the change. If you want to test the effect of using a person's name on response rates, randomly pick half your email list and start with "Dear customer" while starting the other half with "Dear Mr. Doe". Try another experiment the following time, like using the person's name in the subject line of the email.

# 3.4 Additional response rate improvement techniques

In addition to the direct marketing techniques mentioned above, here are some additional ways of improving response rates to email-based surveys, in priority sequence:

1. By far the most important thing you can do is allow respondents to respond to the survey directly in the email they receive. Unfortunately, this is technically difficult. The best you can do is to embed the first question in the email, usually the overall rating question. Use HTML widgets to do this. They do not get blocked by the common email clients at least at the time this is written. Embedding the first question improves response rates by a factor of 2.5x, in my personal experience. Promoter.io and other software providers have found that it triples response rates. My suspicion is that embedding the first question makes it far less likely that people believe the survey link could be a phishing attack or other security risk.

2. Provide feedback to everyone, not just the respondents. When you have completed the survey and determined the actions, write back to the entire mailing list to let them know their voices have been heard and telling them what you are going to do. Those who did not respond are more likely to answer the next time, and could also be given a way of adding their voices immediately if they do not feel represented.

3. Ensure you have an email contact list that you maintain and use regularly for customer communications. That has two main benefits, one obvious and one less so. First, you will have far fewer emails 'bounce' due to unknown addresses. The second benefit is that customers who read your emails will almost certainly have authorized the displaying of 'pictures' for anything received from your email domain. Outlook and other clients default to blocking

pictures from unknown sources. You should minimize the use of pictures and other graphics in outbound emails in any case, as they present consistency challenges across phone, tablet and PC platforms.

4. Test your outbound email with a set of internal users first, to detect problems. Send some additional test emails to internal users from a non-company email address, to see how they display if an email client blocks anything or automatically puts the email in a spam folder.

5. While I have suggested not using strong incentives, simply thanking people in advance, promising to act and to inform them of the results should be a sufficient incentive for many, and should have a positive effect on response rates.

## Risk of over-surveying

How do you know whether you are over-surveying? There are two main principles. First, you need to provide more value than you extract, which should push you towards short surveys. Second, you need to be planning to act on the feedback, including informing customers about your progress. Remember that over-surveying is about individuals, not companies. It does not matter if you send surveys to multiple people in a company. What you want to avoid is sending one individual multiple surveys in a short period of time. When thinking of this, bear in mind that your competitors may be sending surveys to the same person too.

## Over-surveying may be over-rated as a problem

Let's face it, if a customer has not responded to your survey request, they have not wasted any time, but you do not know what they are thinking. Most transactional surveys will give you a response rate between 5 and 15%. Product survey response rates can be a little higher. The people you need to avoid asking to respond again in a short period of time are those who already answered your survey. Most of your customers will not have answered. These should be the focus for the following research round, assuming it happens reasonably soon after the previous one. Write something that starts like this:

## Additional response rate improvement techniques

"Dear Mrs. Smith,

I realize you did not have time to respond to my request to help us improve our product when I wrote to you six weeks ago. The people who did answer helped us to determine the two items below as our top two improvement priorities. I really want to have a third project and would like to once again ask for your help. There are just three questions and this won't take you more than about 3 minutes..."

Taking this approach improves the overall response rate, and therefore improves reliability. Make sure you don't send these emails to people who have already answered.

### More generally

If you have listened to customers, made improvements, then reported the progress back to customers, you cannot be accused of over-surveying if you start the process again. Customers will be able to see that you have provided at least as much value as you have extracted, and will cooperate. It is important to communicate your progress to all customers, not just those who responded.

# 3.5   Does culture affect survey outcomes?

As a person who has lived and worked in seven countries, I believe cultural differences exist and matter. My career has taken me regularly to countries in Africa, Asia, Europe and North America and I have directly observed that people behave differently, especially in business situations. A lot has been written on the subject. My favorite book on the subject is *When Cultures Collide* by Richard D. Lewis[14]. *Cultures and Organizations* by Hofstede and Hofstede[15] is also excellent. I got into the habit of studying the *When Cultures Collide* chapter on a new country before visiting for the first time. I suppose my most educational experience was in Jordan.

Comfort zones in different countries
Along with all the science, Lewis tells entertaining stories about the effect of comfort zones on behavior in groups. In Northern European and North American culture, the 'comfort zone' extends to arm's length. What this means is that people from these cultures become uncomfortable when someone is less than a full arm's length away from them. They will tend to back away from someone the feel has come too close. In Southern Europe, the comfort zone is half that, meaning elbow's length.

Lewis describes multinational meetings, for example European Union social gatherings, where the Southern Europeans back all the Northern Europeans into the corners of the room by the end of the evening. His chapter covering Jordan mentions that the local comfort zone is half again what you find in Italy. He also mentions what happens when you are being successful in your discussions. He was not wrong.

---

[14]   Richard D Lewis: *When Cultures Collide*, 2005, Nicholas Brealey Publishing, ISBN 978-1904838029
[15]   Geert Hofstede, Gert Jan Hofstede and Michael Minkov: Cultures and Organizations, 2010, McGraw Hill Education, ISBN 978-0071664189

# Does culture affect survey outcomes?

## Opening HP's office in Jordan

I went to meet the Minister for Information and Communication Technology together with an American colleague. We wanted to negotiate a series of things to do with opening an office and potentially a software center in Amman. My American colleague had not read the Lewis book, and I did not say anything about what I was going to do in advance. I sat just left of the minister. When the time came to have the critical discussion, I moved to about 20 cm/8 inches from his face, and …this is critical… did not lose eye contact at any time while we spoke. I could see my American colleague getting twitchy while this was going on. And yes, the sign of success then happened. The minister put his arm around my shoulders. We had never met before. My colleague's eyes were popping out. Success! I had learned how to do the male cheek kissing version that is specific to Jordan, but did not get to try it out as we did not socialize beyond the meeting.  On a side note, the best coffee I have ever had in my life was in that office. Something to do with flavoring it with cardamom seeds, I think.

## Exhibit 3.4

Three years of enterprise hardware scores by country for all major vendors

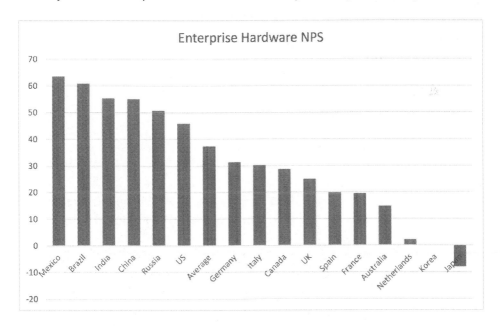

# Survey design

Culture matters, but does it affect customer surveys?

After many years using double-blind surveys at HP and seeing responses that were consistently different by country, I became certain that the sole explanation for the differences was culture. Exhibits 3.4 and 3.5 show what the NPS scores looked like by country for the combination HP and its major enterprise hardware and software competitors respectively, by country. This excludes consumer PCs and printers. The data is for a three-year period and the sample sizes are absolutely massive.

## Exhibit 3.5

Three years of enterprise software scores by country for all major vendors

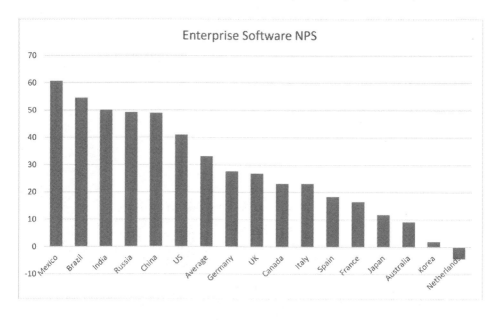

So therefore

The only possible conclusion from this data is that the Japanese, Koreans, Australians and Dutch are grumpy people and don't want to give top grades to anyone. Right? The only possible conclusion? That is certainly what I thought before going to meet Rob Markey for the first time in August 2015. Before getting into what he told me, think about it this way. The data above represents customer views on the major IT suppliers around the world.

# Does culture affect survey outcomes?

Almost all are US companies. Almost all try to do business in other countries exactly the way they do it at home in the USA. Almost all believe that this is the best and only way of doing business and that any other way of doing business is inferior, or perhaps just costs more.

## The perception is widespread

Do a web search on cultural differences in Net Promoter Scores, and you will find a consensus that the cultural differences in scoring are real and look something like the graph above. Even Bain consultants used to agree. Back in 2006, Jayne Hrdlicka, Edmund Lin, Gary Turner, Bruno Lannes, YeonHee Kim and Shintaro Hori published *How to win—and retain—loyal customers in Asia and Australia*[16]. It includes many examples of NPS score ranges from different industries. Most of them have negative average scores. There are also some 'normal' scores in the mix, which should not be possible if the cultural paradigms are 100% correct. By this I mean that either 'all Australians are grumpy when responding to surveys' or they are not. Both cannot simultaneously be true.

## Exhibit 3.6

Per.ceptive NPS benchmarks for Australia

| Industry | NPS | Industry | NPS | Industry | NPS |
|---|---|---|---|---|---|
| Mechanics | 17 | Fast-moving consumer goods | 8 | Plumbers | -5 |
| In-store retail | 16 | Online healthcare stores | 7 | Doctors | -8 |
| Printing | 16 | TV commercial shopping | 4 | Accountants | -11 |
| Hairstylists | 14 | Internet companies | 1 | Security | -14 |
| Whiteware/appliances | 12 | Optometrists | 1 | Event management | -15 |
| Travel agents | 11 | Other financial services | -1 | Hire companies | -17 |
| Insurance | 10 | Dentists | -1 | Online business software | -18 |
| Physiotherapists | 10 | Telecommunication | -2 | Builders | -20 |
| Electricians | 10 | Freight/Logistics companies | -2 | Lawyers | -22 |
| Tutor services | 10 | Painters | -2 | Property managers | -29 |
| Banking | 9 | Landscapers | -2 | Energy companies | -33 |
| Car servicing | 9 | Third-level education | -2 | Distributors | -39 |
| Online retail | 8 | Car dealerships | -4 | Real estate agents | -41 |

---

[16] You can find the Bain study at
http://www.bain.com/Images/BB_How_to_win_loyal_customers_Asia_Australia.pdf.

# Survey design

There is data that supports the existence of cultural differences
Per.ceptive (Customer Monitor) is an Auckland-based company that publishes consumer NPS benchmarks for Australia and New Zealand, among other work. Their work on consumer benchmarks seems to support the 'grumpy Australian' viewpoint. The only other possible explanation would seem to be that all types of Australian companies don't care much about their customers. The report in Exhibit 3.6 is from August 2016.

There is limited though reliable data that says the opposite
If the bar graphs really reflected cultural differences, then there would be no benchmark NPS scores in these countries that would show anything different in any industry. Not only is there in fact benchmark data from the 'bottom four countries' that has similar scores to those observed in the United States, but some of the data is for high-tech. ING Direct Australia scores a 38 in double-blind sampling. Local IT outsourcing suppliers working in Dutch score in the 30s in the Netherlands, though Dutch Telco KPN has an 11.

OK, so these are cultural anecdotes
Here are a few short examples that gradually changed my views about what was going on:

- You should adjust to local conditions if you are not from the country. I remember being beside Francesco Serafini, then the HP Managing Director for Europe, Middle East and Africa, when the CEO of Philips Electronics phoned him. They had recently transferred their IT help desk operations to us. Nobody had told the CEO that one way cost had been reduced was by eliminating Dutch as a language for telephone support. He was angry, to say the least. Angry with us and angry with his CFO who had signed the contract and had not told him about the change.
- According to a former Apple employee I met socially, the Tokyo and Beijing Apple stores had the lowest NPS scores among all stores worldwide, at one point in time. They did deep research into local habits after asking themselves whether the way they did business in New York and San Francisco was appropriate in China and Japan.

# Does culture affect survey outcomes?

The first thing to change was the introduction of 'fast checkout' for a set of commonly purchased items that were put against one wall. The customers could avoid the friendly-but-lengthy typical Apple experience and get out of the store quickly. NPS scores rose to and even above the company average quite quickly.

- I met Bill Thomas of EquaTerra at an IT event. EquaTerra had just published the customer satisfaction benchmark numbers for the Benelux for the IT Outsourcing industry. All multinationals (HP, IBM, Accenture) did badly, and many local providers did very well. I asked him to tell me the top reason why. He said it was because all the local providers had their support teams physically in the Benelux and they all spoke to customers in their languages and accents. The multinationals all operated offshore, providing support in English for the Netherlands and Luxembourg, and non-Belgian-accented French for the Belgian customers. He said this was a pattern in other countries too. The multinationals may have had lower costs, but the costs were quickly forgotten after the contracts were signed.
- A local radio station reported on an esoteric study on how people wanted to be addressed by doctors in hospitals. In the United States and the UK, the vast majority of patients wanted doctors to use their first names. In France none did, preferring their family names. I suspect the answers would be even more extreme here in the French-speaking part of Switzerland where you are expected to know someone before going further than "Sir" or "Madam."
- During a discussion about NPS scores in Australia, a person I met at a Satmetrix conference asked me from where we provided telephone support for Australian customers. I told him it was done from India for the business in question. He told me that many Australian IT companies had tried that, but had moved support back onshore to have people on the phone with Australian accents, despite the cost. HP's consumer support people did something similar when moving UK telephone support back to the UK from South Africa.

# Survey design

## More recent Bain experience

I went to my meeting with Rob Markey armed with my data and convictions. He persuaded me that I was wrong, at least partly. He described his experience working with an unnamed American company's operations in Japan. The Japanese operation had had the worst NPS scores in the company for years. To get a new answer, they asked themselves a new question, "What if the problem is not the supposedly grumpy Japanese? What if the problem is us, and the way we do business in Japan?" That was a transformative question. Bain and their client did deep research on the way Japanese customers wanted to be served. They adjusted the way they did business from top to bottom, and it does not look like any other country. Japan now consistently scores in the top three countries on the corporate NPS chart. Going back to the anecdotes, the company in question had had a policy of always addressing customers by their first names, even in Japan. Totally unacceptable. That was one of the first things they changed.

## Suggestions

What all this means is that cultural differences exist in responses to NPS surveys, and the reasons may not be entirely what you think. At a pure survey level, yes there are cultures that are reluctant to give you the top score. This is a good reason to use the zero to 10 scale for NPS ratings rather than 1 to 5. People who have a cultural reluctance to give you a ten may still give you a nine. There are cultures where customer-centricity has not evolved to the extent it has in the United States. An American company offering US-style service there may do very well compared to local expectations. This may be what we see happening in Mexico and Brazil in the IT industry, for example. There are other countries where behaving in the excessively friendly American way may be totally inappropriate. If I were to suggest remembering one thing when you see low scores in a country, ask yourself, "What if the problem is not the customers? What if the problem is us?" Answer that question before your competitors and you will win.

# Does culture affect survey outcomes?

Communicating multi-country competitive customer experience scores

If you have competitive benchmark scores and graphs like the ones shown above, you should never present them in the way I have. For most companies, competition is local. It does not actually matter much that you and your competitors average an 8 in Australia and a 50 in India. I suggest showing individual country competitive comparisons *without showing the rating scale at all*. Show the tick marks on the graph but no numbers, or just relative numbers compared to your score. What you want in Australia is for your NPS trend to be better than that of your competitors, no matter what the numbers. Comparing country scores to each other mainly wastes time and delays getting on with improvements. Only removing the numbers from the scoring scales can help avoid your audience making irrelevant comparisons.

## 3.6  Learning check

Decide whether each of these statements is true or false. Answers at the back of the book.

1.  Even the font you use in an email asking customers to take a survey can make a big difference.
2.  To make sure you are doing a good job, you should always send a survey request to every customer who phones your service center.
3.  Embedding at least the rating question in a survey request email improves response rates by about 2.5 times.
4.  Culture makes no difference to survey responses, so it is always fair to compare countries' NPS performance with each other.
5.  Low survey response rates tend to give overly optimistic NPS scores.
6.  The more questions there are in your survey, the more likely people are to complete the survey, as it is clearer that you value their opinions.

# 4.    Reliable trusted metric - Part 3: Your CFO is a critical ally

# 4.1 Relationship between NPS trends and revenue

If you work for a for-profit organization, every activity should contribute to your operating profit. If you personally have no credible background in finance, your company Chief Financial Officer is critical to your success. There are two main areas where you must be aligned: proving the relationship between NPS trends and revenue trends, and calculating the lifetime value of a customer.

## Relationship between NPS and growth

You should ask your CFO to assign a person to work with you to validate the relationship between NPS and growth (or decline) in market share. Expect to propose the methodology, and ask that person to assist with the data; both your own and that from your competitors. Organization changes and M&A can make comparisons difficult and a Finance person will be well-equipped to read and understand relevant P&L statements. Assuming you are basing the comparison on NPS data from a reliable benchmark provider, there should be no major difficulty with the analysis. It is natural that you will be able to segment your own data better than that of competitors. NPS trends usually, but not always, predict market share trends. In Bain's experience, NPS trends explain and predict between 20 and 60% of market share trends. While NPS trends are an important growth predictor, they are of course not the only thing that matters. You or a competitor might get distracted by a merger with another company, for example, and that might counteract any NPS gain. There are also types of businesses for which NPS does not provide any predictive value. An example follows.

## Calculating the relationship between NPS and growth

The only reliable basis for calculating the relationship between NPS and growth is a well-executed double-blind benchmark survey. The reason no other survey type provides a reliable data source is because no other research gives you unbiased data on your competitors. Imagine a situation where you only have a single competitor, and you know nothing about their NPS trend. Your own score moves from 22 to 35 over three years. You pat yourself on the back and assume increased market share will follow. Maybe. If your competitor has improved from 10 to 32 over the same period, they will probably take share from you. The thing that matters in the relationship between revenue and NPS is your trend compared to your main competitor's trend. If you are in a highly-fragmented market, it is OK to compare yourself to the overall average.

## Use cubic regression

Since you will not have a huge number of data points for your analysis, cubic regression will normally provide a better data fit than linear regression, quadratic regression or simple correlation. All are easy to test in Excel. Assuming there is a relationship between relative NPS and revenue, a good rule of thumb is that cubic regression will show it to be about twice as strong as a linear fit. An advantage of using multiple regression (rather than correlation), is that you can test the relationship between other factors like an economic recession or GDP changes within your overall model. You can get surprises. The graph below shows the relationship between Net Promoter Score and growth for one HP business, as measured over a period of eight years. The absolute numbers have been modified somewhat from the confidential data, and the trend indications are accurate. Note that the 'data points' line refers to the number of quarters for which data was available. We got 20,000 competitive benchmark survey responses per year.

## Analyzing subsets of a business

Within an overall business, you can and should examine trends for subsets. In one HP Software business, we looked at the effect of NPS trends on license sales, professional services sales, and remedial support contracts. While we found the results somewhat surprising, they do agree with what Fred Reichheld and Rob Markey have found over the years, namely that NPS tends to have little or no predictive value for support / service center types of businesses. My interpretation of this lack of predictive value is that NPS can't predict revenue trends for 'hygiene factor' businesses. These are the businesses that can anger customers, but have no real ability to delight them. Let's discuss each of the three businesses in turn. Exhibit 4.1 shows the results for the overall business. Note that these numbers are not the actual confidential HP numbers, but are all notionally correct.

## Exhibit 4.1

Time lag between overall software NPS and overall revenue changes

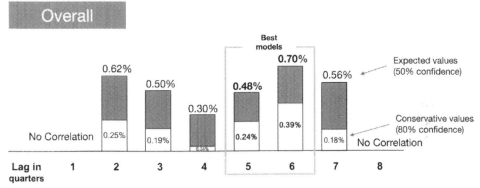

## Exhibit 4.2

Time lag between overall NPS and license revenue changes

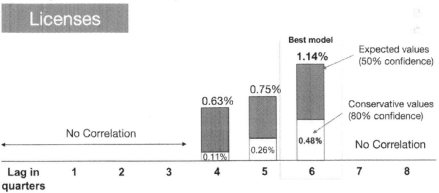

## Licenses

Product purchased follow a life cycle. Customers buy things, and if they are happy they will buy more after some time. In Bain's experience, the average time lag between a movement in NPS relative to competition and a corresponding movement in product sales is about 18 months. Exhibit 4.2 shows approximately what it was like for a major HP software business.

## Professional services

Consulting services include training, installation services and other services associated with using software as effectively as possible. The services are not proprietary, which means customers have alternatives. The effect of this is that changes in NPS produce changes in professional services revenue more quickly and more durably than for product licenses, as can be seen in Exhibit 4.3.

**Exhibit 4.3**

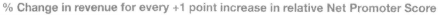

Time lag between overall NPS and professional services revenue changes

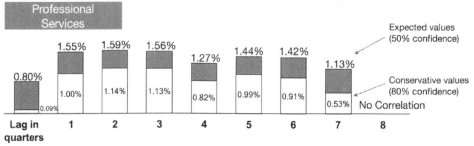

% Change in revenue for every +1 point increase in relative Net Promoter Score

## Support

Reichheld and Markey have long held that the recommendation question is not a good predictor for most support services, meaning services where the perceived value is the ability to call on someone to help you with a product when you have a problem. They don't discuss why. I believe it is because the work of service centers is a hygiene factor. Once it is good enough, there is no real benefit to making it great. The recommendation question works best for products and services that can truly be great. This is what the data showed for HP Software support services, backing up that point. There is no significant correlation between overall software brand NPS scores and software support revenue. Businesses that only or mainly do service center work would be an exception. The non-relationship applies to businesses where the support center exists to do just that, answer questions about a product or service after it has been sold.

# 4.2   Calculating the lifetime value of a customer

While you can find many methods of doing the calculation on the web, there is only one correct answer. The value of a customer to your company is the total cash flow they generate for you over their entire lifetime. The single calculation method for this is Discounted Cash Flow; the Net Present Value of all cash flows out into the future. No other method is correct, though there are some acceptable approximations. The theory and experience of NPS practitioners is that the operating profit per customer is highest for Promoters and lowest for Detractors. Do not confuse revenue and operating profit. You can have customers that generate lots of revenue, but even more cost. They have negative lifetime cash flow, unless you can turn them around.

The main problem you will face
Unfortunately, most companies are not able to calculate profitability by customer. Financial reporting usually works by product line, not by

customer. Asking your finance person to provide you an accurate cash flow from each of your top 100 customers individually will probably be a waste of time. Businesses that depend on large contracts are an exception, and you may well be able to calculate the cash flow from each contract.

### Suggested method

In the absence of accurate standard reporting, a good starting point is to work with your finance person to calculate a 'proxy P&L' for each of your different customer categories. Unfortunately, there are accepted accounting standards for many things, but not for the precise methods used to calculate the lifetime value of a customer. Segmenting customers in a useful way is a critical step. The first distinction to be made is between customers who have an ongoing contractual relationship with your company, and those who buy things, but have no contractual relationship. The former category is easy to work with. Past contract renewal rates can be used to determine future expectations. Direct Marketing principles need to be applied to the latter category. Direct Marketers think in terms of 'RFM': Recency, Frequency, and Monetary value.

Other customer segmentations that are useful will depend on your business model. If you sell both direct and via resellers, lifetime value expectations will be different. They will also differ between very large customers who depend on your company to run their business, and others. If you have the data, NPS categories can be used to refine renewal rate expectations. Here are examples of what needs to be used in the calculation:

- List prices.
- Contra-revenue, meaning discounts you give from the list price. While large customers tend to attract higher 'standard' discounts, you will generally have easier discount negotiations with Promoters than with Detractors. Since contra-revenue is not part of any standard P&L, it is often forgotten.
- Net revenue, meaning list price less contra-revenue.
- Cost of Goods Sold. This includes costs of 'free' replacement items and additional merchandise that you may have to supply Detractors to help turn them around. If you have a dedicated escalations team,

you can easily calculate the average cost per escalation and use that to assign a total escalation labor cost. While 'Cost of Goods Sold' sounds like it should include the cost of selling and marketing, it does not. Selling, General and Administrative costs are 'below the line', which means they are not counted in the Gross Margin calculation, but are considered when calculating operating profit.

- Where Detractors or Passives leave you sooner than Promoters, you can assign a cost of attracting a new customer. Many sales teams are split into 'Hunters' who go after new customers and 'Farmers' who develop deeper relationships over time and are measured on retention and additional business for existing customers. Farmers generally cost about a quarter of the Hunter cost per revenue dollar. If you don't split your sales teams this way, agree a reasonable rule of thumb with your finance partner while you try to measure it more accurately. Marketing costs can be split that way too.

- If you happen to have any indication that you get some of your new customers by referrals from your happiest existing customers, it is worth agreeing a way of taking this into account. However, if you already have a strong enough differentiation between Promoters, Passives and Detractors for your purposes, I suggest this simply be listed as an additional factor that you have not yet quantified. Attaching a reliable number to it can be tricky.

- Beware of the law of small numbers. If the most positive and negative numbers come from unusually small groups in your analysis, you should find a way of combining them with a larger group until you can validate the reality of what you have seen.

If you are not able to get to this level of detail, calculating expected lifetime revenue per customer is a lot better than doing nothing.

If you can only work on one thing for a contract business

If all this is too sophisticated for the time you have available, here is the single area you should focus on, if your business depends on annual contracts. Just agree the value of a one-percent improvement in contract renewal rates. It is easy to calculate, and you probably have the data on past renewal rates. If you work in a large company, you have de facto experiments in place. By this I mean you can simply observe different measurable business practices or levels of customer-centric performance that have happened by accident, rather than by design. Look at how they have affected renewal rates. If you seem to have nothing relevant, test new practices in part of your company and compare renewal rates. You can test multiple things simultaneously, provided you keep a control group, where nothing has changed. Improved renewal rates were how we justified Customer Success teams at HP Software. These teams worked with customers, free of charge, to make sure they were using software effectively and achieving the benefits they expected.

## Summary

Compared to the others, Promoters stay with you longer, buy more products, escalate less, are less price sensitive and are less expensive to sell to and service. There are many businesses that have marginal overall profitability. If you have customers that have been generating negative margins for some time, you will have to decide whether you can turn them around or whether you should drop them as clients. Clarity is more important than always getting the answers you would most like to hear. Once you have agreed the lifetime values of the different NPS customer categories, you and your CFO (or delegate) should present it together to your leadership team for approval. Even if you are not able to do it right away, it should be part of your formal NPS implementation plan. Your credibility depends on it. Your company's long-term commitment to NPS also depends on it.

## 4.3  Learning check

Decide whether each of the following statements is true or false. Answers are at the back of the book.

1. The cost of renewing an existing contract is typically one-tenth the cost of acquiring a new customer.
2. If your overall brand NPS trend is better than that of your competitors, it is safe to assume that all parts of your business will benefit in the same way.
3. Bain experience suggests that the average time lag between a relative NPS improvement and new product revenue improvement is 6 to 18 months.
4. Since contra-revenue is not in a standard P&L statement, it should not be considered when calculating the lifetime value of a customer.
5. To avoid bias, all customers should be considered equal in your research, no matter how much they spend with you or your competition.

# 5.   How not to have a reliable trusted metric

# 5.1 British Airways

While I am sure it is not their intent, the way British Airways surveys both its general and special customers is the worst I have ever seen from any company, from a customer perspective. Perhaps paradoxically, it is one of the richest possible from an internal British Airways perspective. It provides them with a rich set of reports and metrics. While it includes part of the Net Promoter System, it has far too many screens and questions. I have taken their surveys a number of times. I have never seen anything from them about what they have learned and what they plan to improve. They have never contacted me about my issues or improvement suggestions. What follows is a critique that includes screen captures from their September 2016 Executive Club survey. Please bear in mind that I am not entirely negative about it all. I just feel it works from an old paradigm, is internally focused, and designed primarily to fit customer experience strategy and reporting software supplied by KPMG Nunwood.

Summary

While the covering email from Nunwood says the survey will take 15 minutes, there are 134 screens to go through, and it is hard to see how it could be done in 15 minutes. The survey invitation is signed by James Hiller, with no job title. A Google search indicates he manages the Executive Club. Nothing is said about what they have improved based on past surveys.

As distinct from a pure survey about the Executive Club itself, competitors are also covered, as are BA and competing airlines. The huge amount of data collected probably fits a comprehensive internal reporting structure, and provides no particular value to customers. It violates the fundamental principle of customer research in that it fails to provide more value than it extracts. Here is how it starts:

# How not to have a reliable trusted metric

*Cher Monsieur Fitzgerald,*

*Given that you are an Executive Club Member, we would welcome your views on your experiences with British Airways and we would like to understand how they have influenced the way you feel about us.*

*Whether positive, neutral, or negative, your feedback is welcome and highly valued, as it will help us to shape our products and services in the future, and understand what our most valuable customers need from us.*

*The survey will take about 15 minutes to complete.*

Will I be able to provide the input I want to provide?

Before starting to work through the many screens, I decided what I wanted to say. I wanted to make three points:

1.  Transiting through Heathrow Terminal 5 for long-haul travel from Geneva is far more complex than transiting via Zurich, Munich, Frankfurt, Amsterdam and even Paris. This is because passengers have to go through a pointless duplicate security check inbound from the USA / Canada, and a pointless duplicate outbound check when arriving from countries that use the same security standards as the UK. This is because they are unable to separate the 'clean' and 'not quite so clean' transit passengers from each other. British Airways designed the terminal so it is their fault. (Even I have been able to come up with a design that would separate the North American inbound passengers from the rest within the existing layout. The solution is like what has been done in Terminal E in Zurich.)

2.  It is next to impossible to use the Executive Club website to reserve some long-haul destinations using miles. Entire months have no availability. I am not talking about high-demand routes like Christmas in Australia. My latest experience with trying to reserve Australian flights in Business Class was for October, seven weeks

in advance, and there were no flights on any date, either to Sydney or Melbourne. December and January show no availability either, which is less surprising. During a Christmas vacation, I looked at availability for South Africa the following Christmas. Nothing.

3.  I wanted the opportunity not just to complain, but also to make improvement suggestions. Among the suggestions, I wanted to be able to mention that BA should tell us what they are doing with the input, and should contact people who make suggestions.

The short answer is that I was indeed able to provide the input. The more complete answer is that I was forced to bury this critical information inside many unimportant and irrelevant (to me) answers. I am sure the 100+ irrelevant answers correspond to the way some staff inside British Airways are measured.

## The start

I expected BA to provide a choice of languages for the survey, and they do. I suppose it is a bit surprising that Spanish is not among the languages. It is the second-most common first language in the world with about 400 million speakers, after Chinese, with 1.2 billion.

## Exhibit 5.1

British Airways Executive Club NPS questions

Firstly, please think about all that you know about British Airways. On a scale of 0 to 10, where 0 is "Not at all likely" and 10 is "Extremely likely", how likely are you to recommend British Airways to a relative, friend or colleague?

| 0 Not at all likely | 1 | 2 | 3 | 4 | 5 | 6 | 7 | 8 | 9 | 10 Extremely likely |

Still thinking about all your experiences of British Airways, please tell us what it is about those experiences that have left you feeling this way.

Where relevant, please provide details of experience that have left a big impression on you - either good or bad

> The flight experience is good. Terminal 5 is the most frustrating of the major European airports for transit. BA designed the terminal and is responsible for the fact that we need to go through a completely pointless second security check when transiting to and from the USA. It is clear that this is because no effort has been made to separate those arriving from countries with good security checks from those with deficient checks. I avoid LHR for this reason, transiting (from Geneva) via Zurich, Munich, Frankfurt, Amsterdam where there are no transit checks, or even Paris where there is no outbound check.

# How not to have a reliable trusted metric

## NPS questions

The recommendation question is next as shown in Exhibit 5.1. Oddly the 'overall satisfaction' question is asked as well. After a question about emotions, the NPS "Why?" question is asked.

Logically, the following question should be about what BA should improve. That question is never asked about British Airways, though it is asked about the Executive Club, close to the end of the survey. When you do not ask for improvement suggestions, you tend not to get any from Promoters. Remember that Promoters are the customers who admire you most, and want you to succeed. They tend to provide the most valuable improvement suggestions.

## Lots more questions

Questions about my feelings about the airline follow. I suppose these provide overall statistics and somebody is measured on the trend. It is hard to see how someone would work directly on improvements from the answers, as there is no opportunity to explain the input. The questions all use rating scales and include:

- How likely would you be to travel with British Airways in the future?
- To what extent do you consider British Airways a convenient option when choosing an airline to fly with?
- Taking everything into consideration, overall how satisfied are you with British Airways?
- How satisfied are you with the value for money British Airways offers?
- How would you say you feel about British Airways?

## Information about competitors

A useful section follows as shown in Exhibit 5.2. After asking what airlines I have used for long- and short-haul travel in the last 12 months, the survey goes on to ask which airlines are my top choices for such travel. It then asks why the first-choice airline is in first place. I consider this section to be the only thing that is potentially useful beyond the basic NPS questions.

## Exhibit 5.2

BA Executive Club question about competition

You said you would prefer to fly with Swiss, when travelling long haul (5+ hours).

Thinking about Swiss, any experiences you may have had the the feelings towards them, can you tell us in as much detail as possible why you would prefer to fly with Swiss over any other airline?

> (1) No second security check when travelling via Zurich. (2) Very short transit times in Zurich. (3) Convenient flight times from Geneva. (4) Very low short-haul fares for private travel, much lower than BA to London, for example. (5) I like the business class seats in the new 777s.

Oddly, they sort of throw this away by asking you to choose from a list of possible responses for not flying with BA. None of the preselected reasons was my main one, so I filled in the Other box. I feel they should have asked this as an open text question.

Then you are asked again about your overall satisfaction with BA. You can't see the answers to prior questions and my second answer to the same question was one category lower than the first. Maybe because the survey was making my opinion more negative. The wording of the question was not exactly the same as the first one, though I don't recognize them as different questions.

## Lots of rating questions

A seven-point scale is then used to gather answers on flying touchpoints, emotions associated with BA and opinions about their communication. Finally, the section on the Executive Club starts, at last. Remember that the email invitation came from the head of the Executive Club, not the head of British Airways. Overall satisfaction and recommendation questions are followed by another extensive batch of seven-point rating scales Each rating question is presented individually, and you can review your answers to each section, possibly making changes.

# How not to have a reliable trusted metric

## Finally finally

A breath of hope is provided by the question "And finally, thinking about your experiences of any frequent flyer programmes, how could British Airways Executive Club be improved?" I mistakenly thought this was the last question. Unfortunately, I was then asked seven questions about demographic information that BA should already have in my Executive Club profile. This is one of the disadvantages of subcontracting surveys. The confidentiality agreement you have with your customers probably forbids you passing their details to a third party. However, the way BA has handled this with Nunwood is not optimal. Since they already had my name, there would be no reason not to provide them with a unique code, that would then allow BA to match my name and demographic details with their own database. The name on its own might be a duplicate.

## Speculation and conclusion

I recommend a visit to the KPMG Nunwood website at www.nunwood.com. Their offers include customer experience strategy, journey mapping, NPS support and other comprehensive approaches to improvement. One of the approaches, the 'Six Pillars' explains their satisfaction surveys. The excessive number of questions satisfies the needs of the Six Pillars model, and fully exploits their Fizz reporting software.

I speculate that the survey and software are part of a larger consulting engagement with British Airways that requires a 'slice and dice' approach to data for distribution to a variety of internal departments. I feel this is an internally-focused way of proceeding. I would love to know what their response rates are, and speculate that they are under 10% overall. I suppose that higher-status members will be more likely to give feedback, and their input is critical, since they generate the most revenue for the company. I believe an interesting opportunity would be lower-status members who have higher status on other airlines. My recommendation for BA is an A/B split test, asking just the basic few NPS questions as a 'pulse' survey in between the main ones. I believe they would get better response rates and clearer actions to prioritize. Of course, they would lose the 'slice-and-dice' metrics they probably use to measure people.

# 5.2   Audi, and a supermarket

I suppose I should start by saying that Audi is far from being the only car manufacturer doing what I am about to describe. It seems to be a standard practice for car brands.

## Buying a car

Following her purchase of a new Audi, my daughter received a survey request from her salesperson. He provided the link, and added a covering note saying, "Please contact me if you cannot give me a 10." I was surprised to see evidence of this horrible practice reaching European car dealers. It is the rule, rather than the exception in the USA. The General Motors head of customer experience explained it in a pubic seminar. Sales people typically need to average over 95% satisfaction in the GM dealer surveys to be able to participate in their bonus scheme. One low score can require ten perfect scores to even it out.

David Mingle, Executive Director, North American Customer Experience for GM said that he knows this and is not going to do anything about it. He said he personally pays no attention to the scores, only to the written comments. He says customers tend to be honest in their written comments. The sales people are only measured on the scores and don't care what the customer writes about the experience. This is clear evidence of a research process that provides no value. If individual dealerships and sales people have no motivation to read and act on the comments, why should a customer answer the survey at all?

## Consequences

While this may seem to be an interesting anecdote, though backed by facts, it has major consequences. These consequences are evident in the USA and will come to Europe too. In the USA, car prices are considered to be highly negotiable. There are plenty of websites that give advice about how much a

General Motors franchisee has to pay for a particular car, providing the customer with the lowest possible price. I invite you to do your own searches. You will easily find suggestions to use the survey score as a price negotiation point. It is attractive in that the cost to the sales person of lowering the price is zero, while the benefit of a 10 may be high, and costs you nothing. If car companies internalized this, I believe they would change their bonus systems. Indeed, if you receive messages saying "If you can't give me a 10..." during a negotiation process, you should probably negotiate a little more, no matter what it is you are buying.

### Not the only defect in their survey

The Audi survey is somewhat strange. I feel they do not understand the difference between something that matters and something that makes a competitive difference. Exhibit 5.3 shows the way their US dealer survey from a couple of years ago describes what a 10 means:

**Exhibit 5.3**

Part of the Audi survey

| | Unacceptable | | Average | | | Outstanding | | | Truly Exceptional | |
|---|---|---|---|---|---|---|---|---|---|---|
| | 1 | 2 | 3 | 4 | 5 | 6 | 7 | 8 | 9 | 10 |
| Ease of looking at dealer's inventory (well organized, vehicles parked for easy access, etc.) | | | | | | | | | | |
| Variety of inventory (selection of colors, options, etc.) | | | | | | | | | | |
| Comfort of the area or office where you agreed to the price of your vehicle | | | | | | | | | | |
| Appearance of facility (design, cleanliness, etc.) | | | | | | | | | | |

It is not appropriate to label intermediate numbers in rating questions, just the extremes. Personally, I find the difference between "Outstanding" and "Truly Exceptional" hard to understand, let alone worthy of a three-point difference. I also consider the appearance of the facility to be a hygiene factor. Once it is good enough, it has no impact on your purchase. I don't see how it could be a motivator. The same applies to the "comfort of the area or office where you agreed to the price of your vehicle." What is the added value in getting a score above a five, for example? Indeed, perhaps it should be uncomfortable so you want to negotiate quickly and leave.

Of course many other companies do the same thing. According to employees at Walmart, Old Navy, Staples and Best Buy, they are measured on receiving 10s and interrogated about receiving anything less. Exhibit 5.4 is what one US supermarket allegedly gave customers with their receipts:

## Exhibit 5.4

Given with the supermarket receipt

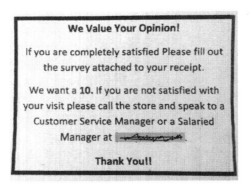

Conclusion

There are many ways to cheat or bias your feedback system. This is just one. For a number to be credible, the people who are asking you to fill out

## How not to have a reliable trusted metric

the surveys must have no direct motivation to achieve a specific score. They should only be motivated by the desire to improve.

# 6.   How to almost have a reliable trusted metric

## 6.1  AppDynamics

A company with industry-leading NPS performance and a customer-centric culture can ruin their message by exaggerating, providing misleading information, and 'comparing apples with oranges'. When you are performing well, there is no need for such communication. What follows is an example of an over-enthusiastic marketing department using an internal NPS result to (presumably not intentionally) misinform customers. It provides a wonderful example of messaging that gets ahead of the actual facts.

The press release

AppDynamics is a company that provides software for managing computer systems. They have recently been acquired by Cisco. Unfortunately, they have become masters of misleading communication about NPS scores. They have repeatedly published silly press releases that discredit their excellent performance and have the potential to discredit the Net Promoter System. In September 2015, they led with this headline:

### AppDynamics Continues With Category-Leading Net Promoter Score of 85 for the First Half of Fiscal Year 2016

More than 500 customers weigh in to confirm positive experience with Application Intelligence Platform

They go on to say:

> *AppDynamics, a leading application intelligence company, today announced that it achieved a Net Promoter Score, or NPS® Score, of 85 for the first six months of its fiscal year beginning February 1, 2015. AppDynamics has maintained an NPS score over 80 for each*

*successive six month period over the last three fiscal years, demonstrating its leadership among enterprise software companies, which on average earn NPS scores of mid-twenties according to Satmetrix.*

And follow that by:

*According to a benchmark study from the Temkin Group, scores for the overall software category in 2014 range from the low teens to the mid-40s. Companies with NPS scores of 60+ are generally considered top performers; USAA (insurance and financial services) and JetBlue are on this elite list, as is Apple. Enterprise software companies have typically had average scores below 20.*

So, what is wrong with this?
Here are the main defects:

- They do not provide any information about the source of the score of 85, though it is implied that it comes from an internal initiative called the Customer 360 program. No other company appears to be covered by that program, so it is not a competitive benchmark.
- They mention the respected Temkin benchmarks without mentioning that Temkin do not include AppDynamics in their data.
- Strangely, they were already well above average for the software industry with scores in the low 40s at the time, according to a double-blind benchmark studies by IPSOS and Qualtrics that I used at HP. The same studies also show IBM, CA, HP and BMC between 40 and 50 for Business Service Management software. The average score for IT management software overall is 38, with 8,800 customer responses. 175 people responded for AppDynamics. VMware was leading at 59.
- While software industry benchmark scores have improved markedly since September 2015, 85 was not a credible benchmark score at that time. No company on the planet had ever had a score of 85 in any double-blind benchmark survey in any industry by the end of 2015. I have personally validated the methodology Qualtrics uses with

Bain and it corresponds to their views on how double-blind benchmarking should be done. I shared the benchmark scores with various competitors before I retired from HP earlier this year. We discussed the AppDynamics press releases too. Some competitors had commissioned their own benchmark surveys, and found similar results to what I mention for AppDynamics. Nobody found scores higher than 45 at the time.

- The software industry has been improving, and here in 2017 it has become more credible that such high scores are possible. I have no doubt that the Customer 360 program is making a difference. My former colleagues tell me that AppDynamics has produced the highest benchmark scores seen. They and their competitors have all improved. It will be interesting to see how this trends.

## Temkin benchmarks

For the sake of completeness, Exhibit 6.1 shows the Temkin NPS technology industry benchmarks for 2016. 62 vendors are covered, almost all of them software vendors. Even without the intermediate points on the table, you will quickly see that the AppDynamics statement that "Enterprise software companies have typically had average scores below 20" is simply not true. Note that the full Temkin report is available for $695[17]. Of course the AppDynamics statement could be based on yet another unattributed source.

## Conclusion

When they had great performance, the sort of press release, website content and sales material AppDynamics used in 2015 did it a disservice. Don't publish scores from your own company surveys and represent them as objective benchmark comparisons. Your competitors know the numbers are wrong and many can easily provide your customers with correct data. The correction may call into question other claims you have made about your

---

[17] The Temkin NPS report on tech vendors is available for purchase here:
https://experiencematters.wordpress.com/2016/09/14/report-tech-vendor-nps-benchmark-2016-b2b/

products or services. If an NPS number appears to be too good to be true, it is!

**Exhibit 6.1**

Temkin tech vendor NPS benchmarks

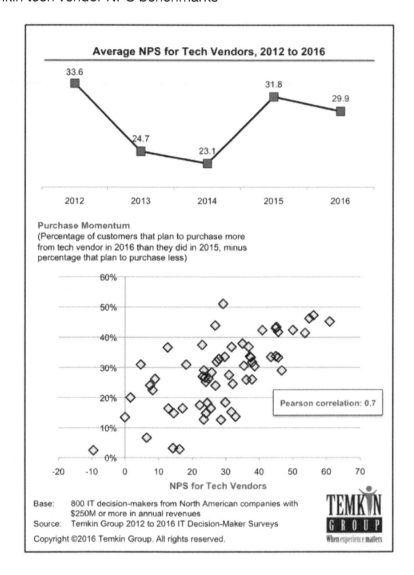

# AppDynamics

If you persuade your senior management that the comparison is fair and real, you also put your future work at risk. After all, your mission seems to have been accomplished. The work should now be put into business-as-usual mode and the investment scaled back. As it is, AppDynamics is on a path to market leadership, though perhaps not at quite the speed their communications people believe. Perhaps this is why Cisco acquired them in early 2017. Finally, note that in the spirit of fairness, I wrote to the person whose name was on the press release to make these points, and he did not reply.

# 7. Feedback, learning and improvement

# 7.1   The heart of the system

While it is unfortunately the only part of the system that many companies use, the NPS numbers don't matter all that much. What matters is what you do with what you have learned. The heart of the Net Promoter System lies in the three processes that support feedback, learning and improvement. They are shown in Exhibit 7.1. The Inner Loop covers improvements for individual customers. You will find that some issues come up repeatedly and need to be improved for many customers. These 'class issues' are the subject of deeper analysis and improvement work in the Outer Loop. The Huddle is a regular team meeting to discuss progress. For those not familiar with American Football, the Huddle is the brief get-together each team does to plan its next play. It takes seconds. Implementing each of the three elements well should be the top priority for your Net Promoter System implementation.

**Exhibit 7-1**

Feedback, learning and improvement

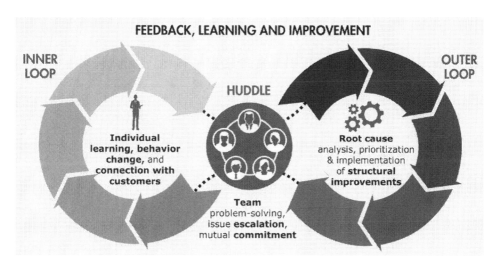

# 7.2   The Inner Loop

Your reliable trusted research process produces feedback that individual employees and teams need to understand and react to. Let's consider the simplest and most common use of the Inner Loop: transactional surveys. A service agent in your technical support team has just finished a call with a customer and closed the incident in your CRM system. The system automatically sends a feedback request to the customer. (The service agent has of course told the customer to expect it.) Surprise, the customer says their problem was not solved, but they were able to find a different way to solve it on their own. First, this feedback needs to go directly back to the agent concerned. Personally, I feel it should go back without human intervention if possible. I don't see a reason that the agent's manager would need to know, depending on how the agent reacts of course. While I have picked an unsolved problem as the example, the agent should get all positive, negative and neutral feedback directly.

Follow up with the customer

Ideally the agent or his / her peers or manager should follow up with the customer to thank them for the feedback, no matter what it is. The call should happen within 24 hours, preferably much more quickly, before the customer forgets about what they have written. Unfortunately, most companies say they are not able to afford the ideal process and only call back the Detractors, at best. (I can't count the number of Detractor responses I have given to Air France and Sabena surveys without ever being contacted in any way.) If you have made the (bad) decision that you can only afford to call the worst Detractors, start with just those who gave you a zero or 1.

There is no formal script for such calls. You need to apologize, then have a discussion. Apologizing works, and you must do it on behalf of the company. "I am sorry we screwed up." not "I am sorry they screwed up." Whatever your cost limitations, you must at least thank every customer who took your survey for doing so. Even if you use a standard email for this, it should come from the head of the appropriate department and give examples of improvements that have come from prior customer feedback. The department head's email and phone number should be included, with an invitation to call or write. That won't cost much and at least your angriest customers get a way of sharing their anger directly with you, rather than just spreading it across the Web.

### No call-back script? Really?

It is obvious when people are speaking to you from a script. It comes across as insincere. You need a formal or informal expert system for the unscripted call-back dialog to be consistent and provide value. The best informal system is coaching from a supervisor, supplemented by discussions with teammates doing the same type of work. Team-mates can help during live calls if you have an instant messaging system. "Let me just check whether any of my colleagues have seen this." Then a short message to the WhatsApp or Slack group for the team, for example. I have also seen this work in a small software development team where the person taking the call would simply (and audibly to the person on the line) talk to a more expert person near them to resolve the situation.

### Don't be afraid to over-recover Detractors

When I joined the DEC Software Product Group in Geneva, we had to travel regularly to Boston. There were no direct flights, and we tried a variety of airlines. The team favorite quickly became the relatively new Virgin Atlantic. To get to Boston, we transited via London's Gatwick airport. We all loved the airline's 'Upper Class' and were rabid promoters, often asking other colleagues why they would go any other way. I am sure we contributed lots of money to the Virgin bottom line.

After about a year of this, one of my colleagues, Peter van der Moosdijk, had a relatively serious incident. His flight from Boston to London was delayed for three hours due to a technical issue. Virgin realized that it was the middle of the night back in Europe and handed out a form for each passenger to fill in, saying whom they wanted Virgin to contact in the morning and what they should say. Peter filled out his form, and boarded the delayed flight happy that his wife would know that he was going to miss the connection in London and would take a later flight.

He phoned home on arriving in Gatwick, and spoke to his panicking wife, who had been to Geneva airport to pick him up, and had heard nothing. The following day, Peter wrote a (paper) letter to Virgin's CEO, Richard Branson, recounting what had happened and saying that this was not what he had grown to expect. Three things then followed. I particularly like the first:

1. A few days later, the doorbell rang while Peter was at work and his wife was at home. Virgin had sent her a huge bouquet of flowers and a card with an apology. I feel this demonstrated a rare level of insight about who actually had the problem. Not their customer.
2. The following day, a letter arrived, apparently signed by Richard Branson (or someone who could copy his signature). He said that what had happened was unacceptable, and that he had sent a copy of Peter's letter to every Virgin office in the world to ensure it would never happen again.
3. At the time, Virgin was the only European airline with a frequent flyer program. Peter's account was credited with enough miles for his family to go on vacation in California the following summer.

Now that's over-recovery. Rather than talking about the negatives, Peter, his colleagues and friends all wound up being Promoters, telling this story over and over again. Our manager even attended a customer experience event hosted by British Airways. He asked whether any of the BA people had flown with Virgin and they had not. Then he told the story. Silence in the room.

## Calling Promoters back

If a customer has told you they would definitely recommend you and that the latest transaction has made this even more likely, you need to have a ready way of activating them; meaning letting them actively promote you. In many businesses, you could simply thank the customer and say you would really appreciate it if the customer could write a product review on a specific website. You may also like to invite them to join your user group or give them a free ticket to a company event. Transactional feedback comes mainly from end users of products and services. In B2B situations, they will not normally be the ones making the purchase decisions. End users have a more direct impact in consumer businesses.

## Why talk to Passives?

In businesses where the cost of change is high, Passives are the category that are most likely to leave you. This is the case for B2B companies that sell things on the basis of an annual contract, or who have dominant market shares in some area. While that may seem surprising, there is a certain logic to it. Passives normally represent about 40% of your customers. You tend not to talk to them much, if at all. The Detractors get lots of attention and often wind up happy. The Promoters are people we like to talk to because they love us.

The Passives? The typical attitude of most companies is "Well, they are not complaining, so I am sure everything is going just fine. No need to talk to them." If you have any competitors, this is a disaster. You have to assume that your competitors are already talking to your Passive customers, and being particularly nice to them. If you seem to have forgotten about them, they will leave you. Of course you can try to stand that on its head, work out which of your competitors' customers are their passives, and start to talk nicely to them.

## If you don't have the resources to talk to everyone

How should you prioritize follow-up if you do not have enough people to call everyone?

- Your top priority should be the people who have provided long responses to the verbatim questions. They care. They have taken a lot of time to provide thoughtful input. You should take at least as much time to call them back and discuss their input. Anyone who provides lots of suggestions is a potential Promoter, regardless of current status.
- The second priority is your Detractors.

Of course, if you don't have the resources to call anyone back, you really should not be surveying.

### Email and instant messaging for collaboration

Many teams use email to discuss and resolve complex customer situations where people outside service center operations have to get involved. It is not a great solution. Email makes it difficult for people who have just joined the conversation to catch up on what has happened up to then. The use of CCs in email chains may mean that no single individual has the full picture. Sophisticated instant messaging systems like Slack may help if you want to be able to view and search the entire conversations easily. It is tricky to find a good balance, as people who only need to contribute something to a small part of the discussion should not have to be notified of every additional message.

## 7.3 The Outer Loop and the Huddle

The Outer Loop is where generic, systematic improvement opportunities get addressed. There are two types of Outer Loop activities:

- The first are those that can be addressed within a single team or function. For example, if your French customers consistently tell you they do not want service center people to use their first names when speaking to them, that can be addressed within the service center.
- The second category of improvement work is that which requires collaboration across different businesses and functions. If your customers tell you that you need to be able to deliver products within 24 hours, when your current minimum is a week, different parts of the company will need to work together to make the improvement.

### Prioritizing Outer Loop work

The essence of any business strategy is the concentration of your scarce resources on just a few things that really matter and help you to beat your competitors. When one initiative is complete, start a new one. For the cross-functional work, I recommend having three to five initiatives, no more. It will make the work relatively easy to communicate and to resource, and the team will see regular progress. The (separate) mono-functional teams should have the same limit. A business or function does not necessarily have to have an improvement initiative. You should not waste resources on things that customers don't care about.

### Useful sources of data for Outer Loop work

Here are the sources of data that are most useful for Outer Loop work:

1. If you have it, the competitive NPS benchmark data should be the most important source. While it might seem subtle, the purpose of

your work is not continuous improvement of everything; rather it is the improvement of a few things that make the biggest difference competitively, whether to catch up, or to provide differentiation.

2. Relationship feedback data is generally the second-most important source to use. If your target customer base is a small number of large companies, it may be all you need.

3. Opportunities that the Inner Loop process has not been able to address are in third place. The reason they are not at the top of the list is that they need to be prioritized in a broader context. While it may seem odd, there will be things a lot of customers would like you to improve but where there is no real benefit in doing so, compared to other potential actions.

4. Operational data is necessary to establish the current state of things customers complain about. For example, your customers may complain about long delivery times for products, and your operational data may confirm that the most popular product was out of stock for two weeks, but it is available now. You may decide to discuss how that situation can be avoided in the future, or may just decide that it was a one-off event. Personally, I totally failed to fix one of these situations at HP, despite trying hard for years. Our manufacturing plants for servers shut down for a week at the end of each calendar year. The order management systems continued to provide customers with estimated delivery dates that did not take the shutdown into account. I tried to get this changed for four years in a row, without success. I believe the root cause of my failure was a corporate function that was being measured by these committed dates, rather than actual shipment dates. And don't get me started on a metric where the 'shipment date' was the day something was put into a shipping container, rather than the day the shipping container actually left.

## Managing improvements — the Huddle

The primary vehicle for the selection and ongoing management of improvement initiatives is the Huddle. The main mono-function Huddles should be weekly or more often, and can be very brief. The majority of their discussions and work need to be on things team members can do on their own. You can complement these by longer meetings on a less-frequent basis. Cross-functional Huddles are harder to coordinate and should be planned as monthly events. The same cross-functional team can have a longer session twice a year to work on the overall customer experience strategy.

## Typical agenda for mono-functional Huddle

Like any other meeting, there needs to be an agenda and people need to prepare for it in advance. Here is a reasonable starting point:

9:00 Welcome — John
9:05 Check status of items on Huddle action tracker — Paul
9:10 New feedback from transactional surveys — George
9:20 Status update on Order TAT initiative — Ringo
9:25 Any Other Business and Close

Fifteen minutes can be plenty for a huddle too.

## A great method for prioritizing work

Jim Dixon of Bain has published a great methodology[18] for prioritizing improvement work. It finally addresses the challenge of making customer journey mapping into something truly useful. Journey Mapping is a popular customer experience technique. Its main disadvantage is that it considers every customer touchpoint as equal. It also fails to distinguish between hygiene factors and things that give you a competitive advantage. Jim's work solves both problems.

## Hygiene factors

A hygiene factor is something like taking a shower: nobody cares if you have one, but everyone will notice if you don't have one for a long time. Think about a real-world example: you don't think about data security when using online banking. You would not recommend your bank because they

---

[18] You can read the Bain description here:
http://www.netpromotersystem.com/resources/toolkit/interaction-prioritization.aspx

did not leak all your personal information and passwords. However, you would certainly be very unhappy if they did.

Jim Dixon takes this into account by considering each touchpoint in terms of its relative ability to delight or to anger customers. The source for this information should be customer comments on the open questions in your feedback system. If Detractors say that long waiting times are the top reason for them being a Detractor, and Promoters never mention waiting times, waiting times only have the potential to anger, and are a hygiene factor.

## Exhibit 7.2

Bain Anger-Delight Matrix

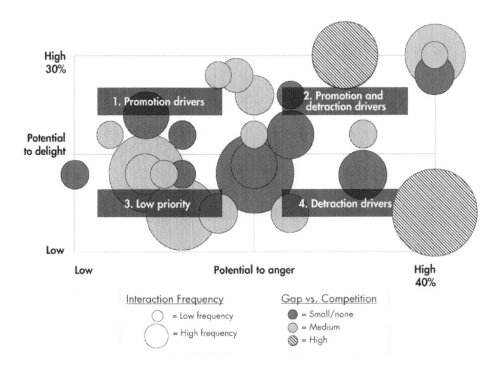

To an extent, this logic is built into the best of the customer journey systems. What Jim adds is competitive benchmarking. This gives you a way of visualizing and taking account of areas where your competitors have an advantage, as proven by your research. Here is the way to combine it all into a single chart. Exhibit 7.2 is from Jim Dixon's work.

## Use in a Huddle

If an Outer Loop team were considering the graph to prioritize improvement work, the two circles with diagonal lines would take top place. This example does not have any green circles, which would be areas where you have a competitive advantage you may want to push even further.

You would probably avoid taking any action on items in the bottom-left box, as your customers don't care about them. Existing 'bottom-left' improvement work can and should be wound up to provide resources to work on the new priority areas. This process should be used to establish the initial 'long list'. A further step is needed to get to the final short list.

## Exhibit 7.3

Ease-impact diagram – Top-right box is best

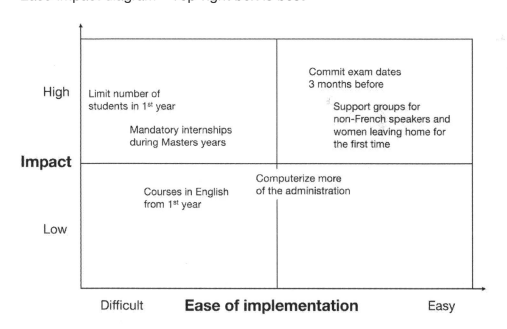

Prioritizing initiatives

Exhibit 7.3 is a simple diagram that will help you to prioritize improvement initiatives based on impact and ease of implementation. In the diagram below, you would get to work on the ones in the top-right box right away. This example is from a survey of Swiss business school students.

# 7.4  Activating Promoters

So, you have identified a lot of Promoters, Passives and Detractors. As humans, we like the sense of accomplishment that comes with putting out fires. It is tempting to spend all our time on Detractors. After all, we understand their problems. We know what to do. As for Promoters, well, it is far less clear what we should do. Here are some examples and ideas.

## Tesla's Promoter program

Tesla is in the fortunate position that a lot of people love their Model S cars. They have taken the principle of activating Promoters to a new high. Existing customers are invited to enter the company's referral program, and receive a referral code. If one or more of their friends or colleagues use the referral code when buying their own Tesla, the Promoter receives ever-increasing rewards. At the time of writing, the rewards are as follows:

- Every referral means an additional ticket in a periodic prize draw for a Ludicrous P90D Model X.
- Two referrals mean a Tesla sports bag.
- Three brings a Tesla jacket.
- New Tesla wheel rims come with five referrals.

# Feedback, learning and improvement

- Promoters get invited to the next major Tesla event after ten referrals.

The top Promoter in 2015 had 188 referrals and won the car. There is a client-side incentive to accept referrals too. If you buy through a referral, you get a $1,000 price reduction. Tesla prices are not negotiable in the showroom, and a purchaser can simply enter the referral code when ordering online, or in the showroom.

## Using an existing platform, or creating your own

Rewarding loyalty from existing customers is relatively easy. My wallet contains everything from Starbucks and Café Nero loyalty cards with sequences of punch holes, to airline loyalty cards. Putting a system in place to encourage your fans to refer their friends can be more complex. There are several online platforms for the work, and I have no particular preference among them. Starbucks, Virgin America, Staples, Lands' End, Microsoft and other companies have used Extole (www.extole.com) for their online referral programs, allowing Promoters to use Twitter, Facebook, email and text messages to share their experiences and link to web pages and social media. Both the referrer and referees are eligible for rewards.

At the simplest level, if you operate at retail level and use a physical loyalty card, one approach would be to give a 50%-off refer-a-friend coupon to each customer who completes a loyalty card. While it is true that the coupon will not necessarily be used for a new customer, the same is true of Extole and other systems for consumer businesses that do not have exhaustive records of all customers.

## Promoters may not have purchasing power

Where your customers are companies, end users of a product or service often have no authority to order from you. They have some influence over the person who can order from you, and you need to stimulate them to exercise that influence. But it may be a mistake to believe that individuals cannot help. Things have been changing radically in high-tech and it is easy to see how the trend is spreading elsewhere. In the old (but recent) days,

132

anyone buying software in a medium to large company had to go through the IT department and they in turn went to procurement. The reason was that you needed new hardware to run the new software, and the IT and procurement people controlled hardware purchases.

Let's suppose you have happy end users of software in a company. You would like them to consider your new product. Ensure it is available in a free version that limits (for example) the number of users. This is how messaging application Slack got started. Individual groups of users that did not have to pay anything spread their enthusiasm to departments and whole companies. Since it is Cloud-based software, no new hardware is required to run Slack. This means that departments can order it online, on their own. At a greater scale, this is also how Salesforce.com grew and beat Siebel. Sales organizations could decide to use Salesforce.com even without the agreement of the IT department, as no new hardware was needed. Of course, whoever was buying still needed a budget.

Conclusion

Promoters are not the only people who should be 'activated' to help you. After all, most people who would like to recommend your company have probably not answered your survey. However, Promoters are a great starting point. You know you can approach them with confidence, since they have already said they are likely to recommend you. Start with Promoters, then talk to others who seem to like your company a lot.

# 7.5 Concentrate on what is difficult

I had been managing projects for over 20 years when I had an unpleasant surprise. I had recently moved to a new manager and met him in his office in Munich. We reviewed progress on my latest project. After about an hour, he looked at me and said, "Maurice, you know nothing about project management." After blustering and arguing that I had been doing it for a long time, so that could not be true, I finally asked him what he meant. He asked me some basic questions, like "What is a deliverable?" and "What is a task?" I did badly in answering. The root cause was that I had never had any formal training in project management. This had consequences. The main one was that I could not communicate effectively with people who had full Project Management Professional (PMP) training. We used the same words, but meant different things. My definitions were wrong and the PMP experts were correct. I fixed the problem by taking a 'light' course.

### Effective communication is the most important thing

If you can get things done, but have never been trained on how to communicate effectively in person and in writing, that should be your next step. After all, unless you are in a manual job, you can only get other people to do things by what you write and what you say. You need to learn to do both well. There are many courses available on speaking, writing and presenting effectively. I would also recommend complementing them by reading both the original Freakonomics book[19], and the outstanding behavioral economics book, Predictably Irrational[20] by Dan Ariely. They will both help you to communicate in ways that differentiate you from the average. In business strategy, being different works just as well as being better.

---

[19] Levitt and Dubner: *Freakonomics*, 2009, William Morrow Paperbacks, ISBN 978-0060731335
[20] Dan Ariely: *Predictably Irrational,* HarperCollins, 2008, ISBN 978-0-06-135323-9

## Concentrate on what is difficult

Getting things done effectively is a close second

Whatever the content of your customer experience strategy, if you and your team are not able to implement it, you are doomed. Once you have decided what to do and committed results to your management, the most important thing is to do it. Professional project management training is essential. Look up 'PMP' on the web and you will find lots of options, both online and in the classroom. If you happen to work in software, I suggest doing project management training first, then talking to your R&D team to see how to enhance project management by adding aspects (such as Sprints) from Agile software development. Clearly, the first and second items on my list are strongly related to each other. It is impossible to get things done if you cannot communicate effectively. Your communication will be wasted if you never get anything done.

## 7.6  Learning check

Decide whether each of these statements is true or false:

- The Inner Loop is where you follow up with customers on individual feedback items. The Outer Loop is where you work across departments on feedback that has come from many customers.
- All common customer improvement suggestions are equally important. You should staff up to work on as many as you can afford to.

# 8.   How not to deal with a Detractor

## 8.1   Nike - losing a customer - me

Nike and Lululemon are probably the two most respected and recommended clothing brands as I write this. What I want to relate is what goes wrong when a brand tries to support a non-core product. The product in question is the running application for iOS and Android called the Nike+ Run Club.

From problem to FAQ to Facebook

I have been using the Nike+ running app for a couple of years on my iPhone and have logged over 1,000 kilometers (600 miles). The Run Club is the latest version, which I currently have on my iPhone 6. I always use kilometers as my units. On the second run with the new version, the displayed number was a distance in miles, but the units displayed were kilometers. My average pace showed as 8 minutes per kilometer, rather than my usual 5. I checked the distance I had run online, and confirmed the nature of the error. First stop, the Nike web page devoted to their applications. Nothing found in their Frequently Asked Questions. A note there directed me to their Facebook page as one support option, saying it works from 9 a.m. to 6 p.m. Pacific time. So, I went there to share my experience and ask for help.

They have apparently not heard of their own app

The Facebook experience was quite surprising. I used their search function to find out whether anyone else had had the same problem. Apparently not. I decided to explain my own. Describing it was not a problem. Using their pull-downs to categorize it was a problem. First, the app was not listed. Since an old version was there, I selected that (the Nike+ Running App), as shown in Exhibit 8.1.

Then I was asked to supply my OS version. As I write this, iOS 10 has been released. Apparently, Nike had not yet heard of iOS 9.

## Exhibit 8.1

Nike support choices

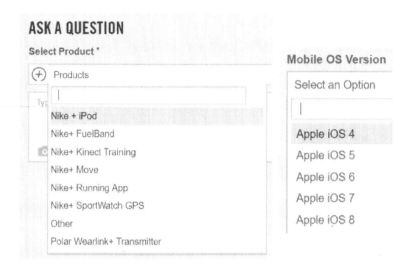

Naturally, the app versions available did not include mine.
- 24 hours later… nothing.
- 48 hours later… nothing.
- 72 hours later… nothing.
- 96 hours later… nothing.

So therefore…
So I deleted the Nike+ Run Club app and installed the Endomondo Sports Tracker app instead. Endomondo is owned by sports clothing manufacturer Under Armour. Your Detractors will leave you if they complain and you do nothing to respond. All my running clothing is from Nike. Will I start to look more favorably on Under Armour gear? Only time will tell.

# 9.    Robust operational and analytic infrastructure

# 9.1 It is about the team and the tools

This part of the framework is about the team and the tools. What sort of team do you need? Where should it report? What tools do you need to conduct research and understand the results? The Net Promoter System research process produces lots of written answers from customers, and indeed from your own people if they interview customers. What can be used to transform all that unstructured information into deep insights? Are you better off with a set of individual tools, or a single comprehensive solution.

Software is in constant evolution

Software is evolving at a much faster rate than the Net Promoter System. The software that is improving most quickly is that used to analyze text responses to surveys. Traditional analysis tools require data to be structured. Text responses are unstructured data. Relatively new techniques such as Natural Language Programing are required to deal with it. I will provide guidelines and an example of how to choose text analysis software. The guidelines should not change, but the answer they provide you will change, as each vendor improves their product.

A second area that is in constant evolution is comprehensive software platforms to manage everything from a customer list, to surveying, routing and tracking follow-up actions, reporting and project management. Some software solutions are integrated into Customer Relationship Management systems like Salesforce.com, and some are standalone. I will only cover this area superficially.

Some NPS areas are mature

There are parts of the system that are mature, and where software exists that does a perfect job. This is the case for the basic research or survey software. Within reason, it is hard to go disastrously wrong. I have my personal preferences, which I explain.

143

## 9.2 Team

Focus produces results

It is easy to say, "Everybody is responsible for the customer". The problem with this statement is that when everyone spends a little of their time on improving things for customers, but nobody does it full-time, nothing is likely to change. If you are already the loyalty leader in your industry, that may not be a problem in the short term. Success in improving customer experience requires a dedicated person or team. That leader must be well-connected and respected in your organization. Where they report does not matter much. The teams of which they are members matter a lot.

## Relationship with sales leadership is critical

If you are successful in measuring and improving customer experience, you will sell more. Your sales team should find that value proposition quite compelling. The customer experience leader needs to have an excellent relationship with sales and should be part of their leadership team. I am not suggesting that he or she should report to the sales leader, simply that they must be in the team. My own approach has been to start by proposing to attend an internal sales meeting to present competitive benchmark data. Sales teams find the insights about their competitive advantages and disadvantages to be really useful, so they have always been attentive. Using that positive feedback, I then propose to be a permanent member of the sales leadership team. That has usually worked for me.

## Reporting lines in larger organizations

In a large organization, each major business should have a customer experience leader. The job title does not matter. Customer Advocacy is used quite often. Personally, I have held a full-time customer experience role reporting to the EVP of Software at HP, and have also combined the job with the Chief of Staff role for other business areas. The Chief of Staff tends to be well-connected, neutral, and controls the leadership agenda. Having editorial control means customer experience can always be part of strategic discussions. If the Customer Advocacy leader is a full-time role, a great relationship with the person setting leadership meeting agendas is important. Customer Experience falls into the general category of things that are important, but not urgent, and can easily become an agenda also-ran.

## Chief Customer Officer role

There are aspects of customer-centricity that cannot be addressed within a single business or function. We have seen the rise of the Chief Customer Officer (CCO) over recent years. The CCO should report to the CEO. The job description should include most of the following areas, depending on the size of your company:

# Robust operational and analytic infrastructure

- Chair and run a cross-organizational Customer Experience Council that shares successes and agrees strategy across your company.
- Define, fund and implement the on-boarding and refresher NPS training that should be mandatory for all employees of all levels, including the executive leadership team.
- Define and implement appropriate NPS measurement and reporting standards across the company.
- Regularly report progress to the Executive Leadership Team.

The only advantage I see with the CCO title is that it is better recognized externally than, for example, the Customer Advocacy Officer title. The job content is the same.

## Customer complaints team

It is a good idea to have a single customer complaints team for your entire organization. The phone and email contact details for complaints should be visible at the top level of your company website. "Log a complaint" is a reasonably clear heading. The person or people should accept complaints from both internal and external sources. It is difficult for complaints team members to be effective if they are new to the company. The ideal profile is a relatively experienced company veteran who understands the organization and can get things done quickly. A single person could do this on a part-time basis in a small company. A team is needed for a large organization. When I managed this for HP, covering consumer and enterprise business, there were over 100 people in the complaints team in Europe alone. We had 350,000 employees in the whole company at the time. The range of work was quite extreme, even including representing the company in small claims courts when people went there to get satisfaction on a printer or PC problem.

The complaints team, and perhaps your full organization, should have the authority to spend a certain amount of money to resolve complaints immediately, without further approval. That amount should be something between $1,000 and $10,000. In HP, the Swiss complaints team could leave the office, go to a local electronics store, buy a product and drive it to the customer's home near Zurich, if that was appropriate. Flowers and other small gifts are a good way of apologizing when you make mistakes or a product is defective. Think about this when you are trying to turn around detractors. Note in passing that most countries have rules prohibiting gifts to government employees, so your processes need to take this into account.

## 9.3  Survey infrastructure

"They left out the infrastructure?"

"Yup. The marketing department's report is considered a creative classic."

Unless yours is a very small company, you will not be able to implement and operate an effective Net Promoter System without appropriate technology. To the extent possible, you should use Cloud-based (SaaS) solutions that do not require you to invest in hardware. Among other things, an advantage of this approach is that you will not be constrained by a corporate IT budget, and can advance on your own. Cloud software is always up-to-date. For the sake of this discussion, Customer Relationship Management software, used by sales and call center people, is out of scope.

Simplest possible research infrastructure
You can use Excel with Outlook mail merge to send surveys, and that can work in small volumes. That should work with Open Office too. The primary challenge is ensuring it looks OK on a phone. Here are the advantages of this simple approach:

- You probably don't have to spend any money to get into motion.
- Assuming small volumes, you can simply ask people to reply to the email to send their survey responses.

- The emails can go directly from anyone you choose, such as a product manager, or from a process mailbox in the name of the product manager.
- If you have designed your survey correctly, customers should be able to see the entire survey on a single screen when they open the email. This is almost impossible when using a link to a web-based survey. When customers see the full survey, it improves their belief in your statement that it will only take them a couple of minutes to respond. That in turn will improve response rates compared to a web link.

There are disadvantages, even in small volumes:
- Managing opt-out lists is difficult. Any survey you send should include a way for the customers to decline the survey and to tell you they no longer want to receive any surveys. If you work from a single Excel contact list, you can probably handle it correctly. If multiple people send surveys from multiple contact lists, it can be difficult to coordinate opt-outs across lists.
- To do any analysis of the results, you will have to copy-and-paste or otherwise transcribe what has been sent back.

### Basic survey infrastructure
Getting beyond the extreme mentioned above, I recommend using SurveyMonkey and MailChimp for basic needs. There are a number of similar alternatives that will also work just as well.

SurveyMonkey advantages:

- There are different levels of monthly SurveyMonkey subscriptions, going from free to advanced solutions with no customer-visible evidence that you are using SurveyMonkey. (Really, they could have chosen a name that would make them sound less like amateurs.)
- Higher subscription levels include simple text analysis.
- It runs in many languages.
- There are 'certified' NPS templates.

- Lots of people use it, so lots of advice is available.
- You can download results as Excel files for your own analysis.
- You can send emails directly from their service.
- If you don't like it, don't renew your monthly subscription.

SurveyMonkey disadvantages:

- If you use a separate email solution, you can only provide a link to the SurveyMonkey survey in your email. There is no way of embedding the rating question in your email, so response rates will be lower (less than half) than with solutions from Medallia, Promoter.io and others that embed the rating question in the outbound message.
- When I say the text analysis is basic, it really is basic. So is Medallia's, at the time of writing.
- Some nice tracking options are only available if you use SurveyMonkey's outbound email service.

MailChimp advantages:

- MailChimp lets you see who has opened your messages and who has clicked on any link they contain. This is particularly useful for A/B testing. By this I mean, for example, sending email with different subject lines to each half of your mailing list to see which subject lines get better open rates, and doing the same for different requests to take your survey. You should only change a single thing at any time to have a valid A/B test.
- If your list has up to 2,000 customers and you want to send no more than a total of 12,000 emails per month, you can do it for free. The paid plan starts at $20 per month for 500 customers, for example.

MailChimp disadvantages:

- MailChimp tracks recipients' actions, but does not disclose that it is doing so, at least by default. I am already aware that this has been raised as an issue with the national data privacy organization in one European Union country.

## More advanced solutions

Two capabilities are the most critical when considering advanced solutions for managing NPS surveys. For clarity, I am talking about software that only manages surveys. There are of course many solutions that manage surveys and many other things too.

- You should embed the rating question in outbound emails to customers. This will give you double to triple the response rate, compared to sending the same survey with just a link in the email. There are various reasons for this. Given the number of phishing and ransomware attacks we hear about, people are reluctant to click on links they do not absolutely trust. It helps if the email comes from your company email server and that this is clearly visible.
- You need to be able to do a first-pass analysis of the verbatim answers without human intervention. More on this and how to select such software in the next chapter.

While many vendors push it hard, I am not a fan of encouraging customers to respond on a phone. The main value you get from NPS research is the answers to the open questions. I feel you should tolerate phone-based text input, understanding that it will be brief. Your outbound email should say something like "You may be most comfortable providing feedback on a PC, Mac or tablet."

# 9.4   Evaluating text analytics software

"So what do I do now?"

The great advantage of the NPS feedback format is that it is short, with a rating question and one or two other open questions. Like most survey types, the purpose is to find out what customers care about and what you need to improve. The main challenge of the open text response format is the need to analyze what people have written, ideally without any human bias. I would like to cover some general principles about using text analytics software, then present a real-world case where such software was analyzed as part of a business-school degree course. The overall intent is to provide you a way of comparing and selecting software for your own use. There is no single universally-correct answer. Your answer will depend on factors like volumes, languages and budgets, among others.

General principles about text analysis software
Here is what I believe text mining and analysis software must be able to do, with increasing levels of difficulty as shown in Exhibit 9.1. Software should be graded in each area:

# Evaluating text analytics software

- Accept inputs in a variety of formats such as Excel, SurveyMonkey, SalesForce, .csv, video and audio files and so on. The more the better.
- Recognize inputs in a variety of languages. Again, the more the better.
- Identify concepts in a meaningful way. There are four levels:
  - The first is simple word frequency, with no filtering. Words like 'the' or 'very' could come up.
  - The second recognizes nouns and discards articles and conjunctions. 'Heart' and 'Attack' would be separate topics at this level.
  - The third level is multi-word topics, such as 'Heart Attack' or 'Cardiac Arrest'.
  - Finally, words that mean the same thing need to be grouped into a single concept. For example, "support website" and "support webpage." This avoids long lists of concepts.
- Identify sentiment to determine whether respondents refer to a concept in a positive, negative or neutral way. Sentiment analysis determines which attributes a customer associates with the concept.
- Identify themes by combining concepts with sentiment and/or linguistic analysis. 'Fatal heart attack' or 'Disgusting undercooked food' might be themes. 'Bad food' is a different theme to 'good food'. This last example illustrates why simple word frequency software is not useful for survey analytics. Just getting the word 'food' a lot will not tell a restaurant owner much.
- Group similar themes to avoid excessive granularity. 'Serious heart attack' and 'Major cardiac arrest' are grouped together in this step. It may involve use of industry-specific libraries or taxonomies. Some software is delivered with such libraries or lets you add your own. Other programs use data-driven approaches to determine similar words based on how your customers use them in a sentence. Google, for example, uses data-driven Natural Language Processing to make sense of your search queries.
- Finally, my experimentation so far has shown that correct handling of pronouns turns out to be very difficult indeed for software, remaining easy for humans. More on the problem later.

**Exhibit 9.1**

Levels of sophistication of text analysis

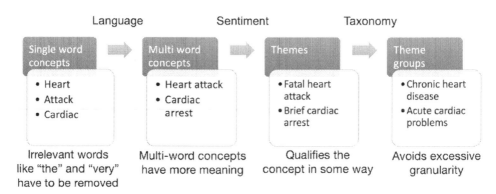

State of play in early 2017

What follows is an example of an actual comparison and evaluation of analytic software. The software evaluated was for a specific need and had to meet specific criteria. Your needs and criteria will be different. It does get somewhat technical. You may like to just skim over it, or jump straight to the results at the end of the chapter.

My daughter Claire did a business school project about text analytics for Net Promoter Score surveys in mid-2016. She got permission to survey all business school students, then used a wide variety of software to analyze the text responses, comparing them with human analysis. The survey was a classical NPS survey. She used SurveyMonkey to send it, and there were three questions, plus demographics.

The questions were "How likely are you to recommend the business school to someone choosing their third-level studies?" "Why?" and "What should the business school improve?" She resisted attempts by others to add rating questions, and the survey results validated this resistance. One of the top suggestions was something that would never have come up using a closed survey.

# Evaluating text analytics software

## Overall objective of any survey analysis process

Unless you are only interested in tracking a metric, for example to reward people, the fundamental purpose of any survey analysis is to find out what your top improvement priorities should be. The winner of any comparison should therefore be the process or tool that answers that question. The advantage of software over humans is that the only bias is that caused by the programmers. I admit that such bias can be considerable, particularly when selecting the algorithms to be used to categorize text.

## A hard historic lesson on decision criteria

In all scientific experiments, it is critical to set up the methodology before you have any data. This was made very evident by changes in US rules on drug approvals. Experimenters are required to provide details of the exact methodology and data analysis process before they start the clinical trials. The results have been dramatic. If you go back 40 years to when researchers could decide how to run the analysis after they had the data, over half the trials were successful. Now the success rate is just under 10%[21], as people cannot remove data or change their analysis after the fact because the results do not suit them.

## The seven-country study farce that affects our lives today

The most famous study that suffered from post-hoc adjustments was the legendary and highly influential 'Seven countries study' by Ancel Keys[22] on the relationship between diet and heart disease by country. The study was done in 1958 and continued for 50 years. It showed a directly linear relationship between saturated fat consumption and heart disease. In 2009, Robert Lustig found that Keys had cherry-picked the seven countries from a data set that included either 21 or 22 countries. He apparently discarded the data from the 15 countries that did not support his theory. A separate piece of work also showed that Keys' results could be better explained by differences in sugar consumption, which Keys had not studied. There is a

---

[21] A Nature Biotechnology article about current approval rates is at
http://www.nature.com/nbt/journal/v32/n1/full/nbt.2786.html
[22] The Wikipedia article on the study does its best to take a neutral position.
https://en.wikipedia.org/wiki/Seven_Countries_Study

nasty history of scientists who took positions opposing Keys losing their research funding and even their jobs.

## Decision criteria for text mining and analytic software

The people at Sift, now called Keatext[23], produced a nice eBook on how to select this kind of software. There is a danger of bias here, in that their own software naturally meets their own criteria. For her study, Claire decided to use some of the Sift criteria, deciding that there were a few factors that did not matter much. The result of her work was these decision criteria:

- The ability to access, read and extract words in common file formats and in multiple languages.
- Show how often topics occur.
- Ability to attach sentiment to topics in a useful way. Useful means that it is easy to understand what the sentiment refers to.
- Ability to group similar topics together, even if the words are somewhat different. This is what allows you to summarize the actions that need to be taken from a survey.
- Ability to refine the selections for reporting purposes.
- Nice graphics and other features that make presenting the results easy.

Each item was scored on a 1 to 6 scale with 6 being the maximum. What can I say? The Swiss education system grades this way, so the scale was natural for her.

## Scope

All software analyzed had to be either free or available in a fully featured trial version, and all had to at least claim to be up to at least some of the task. This led to some notable exclusions, especially commercially available text analysis solutions which we discuss in the next chapter. The trial version of Watson does not do text analytics. She was unable to find NPS

---

[23] The eBook can be downloaded at the bottom of the Keatext homepage at http://www.keatext.ai/

survey analytics examples for IBM's BlueMix software on Github or the IBM site. Here is the list of solutions that are described in more detail below:

- Humans
- Data Cracker
- WordyUP
- Wordclouds.com
- Keatext
- SurveyTagger
- Etuma Feedback Categorizer
- SPSS (from IBM)
- Lexalytics
- MeaningCloud (Excel Plug-In)
- Text2Data (Excel Plug-In)
- Haven OnDemand

## Humans

With all their defects, the baseline for all comparisons was human beings. Some students were asked to scan the survey responses and group the ones they felt to be the most important. Human bias emerged quickly. One of the students looking through the improvement suggestions was French. Several people (presumably trying to be funny) had suggested that fewer French students should be allowed to attend the school. The French student going through the responses insisted that this was the most common suggestion. It was not, and did not appear on the lists given by other students.

Nonetheless, the students were reasonably consistent. Among the reasons for ratings, humans picked the quality of the education as the top reason, followed by the beauty of the campus. Some software agreed. The consensus of the human analysis was that the top suggestion by Promoters, Passives and Detractors was to announce the exam dates earlier. No software available without charge identified this as the top improvement suggestion. Survey responses were mainly in French, with some in English and just one in German. The humans understood all three without difficulty. Priorities for the why and improve questions are shown in Exhibit 9.2 for the first four humans.

## Exhibit 9.2

Human analysis inconsistency

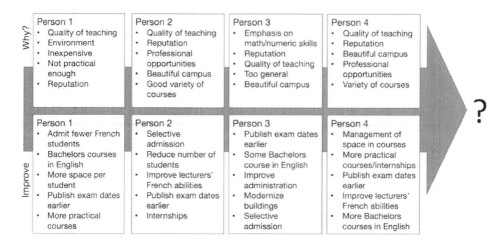

Humans don't scale well

This is one area where the results of the business-school survey may differ from more common needs. The small number of responses meant it was realistic to ask humans to do the analysis. If your needs involve tens of thousands of lengthy responses, using people to do the analysis will be difficult. Humans can review about 15,000 words an hour, and the quality of the work goes down as they get tired.

Main challenge when humans help software

Generally, tagging responses to manually categorize them introduces human bias and is not a good idea. In one part of HP, tagging support survey responses worked well until a second person was needed to handle the volume. Since the two did not agree on the categories, trend data was disrupted. Adding a third person made it worse. You can make manual tagging work if you invest in training.

Here is what humans can do that no software can as yet

Humans can handle pronouns and understand context. Let's consider pronouns first. No software tested could handle pronouns correctly. Take this unrelated example. "The cat walked into the room. It was empty." No software tested could identify what the 'it' was. While it might seem simple to write code to force the software to revert to the prior noun whenever it encounters a pronoun, there are many exceptions to this rule. This brings us to the second thing that does not present any difficulty for humans. Take this example. "The cat walked into the room. It was fluffy." Humans know that fluffy almost certainly refers to the cat rather than the room.

# Empty cat in a fluffy room

Humans are good at recognizing and adjusting for context. Both humans and software would be confused by "The cat walked into the room. It was dirty." Good grammar suggests that the room was dirty, but it is difficult to be certain. I suppose this is tone of the challenges that Natural Language Processing software will need to address in the future.

DataCracker

DataCracker is available at www.datacracker.com. It is free for surveys with up to 100 responses. It works by looking at individual words. It is not able to identify multi-word topics or concepts. It is probably the software that is able to import data from the widest variety of formats. The business-school survey had over 250 responses, so the full set of answers could not be loaded into the free version of the software. You can see a screenshot of the main text analysis view below. It is a typical word cloud, with font size indicating relative frequency. Since it does not understand language, irrelevant words like "la", "les" "très", "et" and so on come out frequently. (The, the, very, and). As with all word clouds, you can see in Exhibit 9.3 that "interesting" is a common word, without any indication of what exactly is interesting. Unlike WordyUp and Wordclouds.com, you can ignore words by clicking them on the list on the right. This of course allows you to bias the results in any way you like.

**Exhibit 9.3**

Data Cracker (free version)

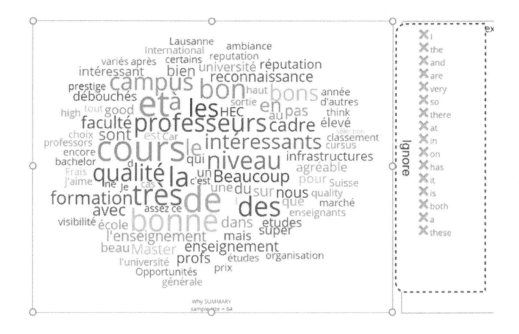

## WordyUp

WordyUp goes beyond the basics of word clouds by showing the relationships between different words. However, the free version at wordyup.com is limited to 500 words. The central challenge the software faces is the same as for many word clouds: irrelevant words like 'because' take priority if they occur frequently, as shown in Exhibit 9.4. At least in the free version, there is no way to exclude any particular word. The only form of data entry is to copy text into the appropriate box on their website. The sample below is from 500 words that were responses to the "Why?" question in the survey. The grouping of words about the campus is well done. Groupings for the improvement question were far less useful.

**Exhibit 9.4**

WordyUp

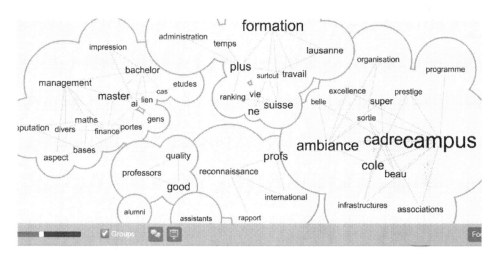

## Wordclouds.com

For pure simple and free artistic word clouds, it is hard to beat wordclouds.com though Wordle produces similar results. Wordle and Wordclouds.com are so similar that it was not useful to include both tin the analysis. The software works on any device that can display HTML. The output can be displayed in a variety of attractive shapes. It treats 'Good' and 'good' as two different words. Words can be excluded manually. You need to exercise caution when using the control slider to resize the cloud, as differing words are excluded from the cloud depending on the size of the graphic you choose to display. Some of the most popular words are excluded in some formats, and there is no apparent reason behind the choices. Words can be excluded or added manually, and the weight of each word can be modified. Exhibit 9.5 shows the output using an English translation of the "Why?" responses.

**Exhibit 9.5**

Wordclouds.com

Keatext

Keatext is another cloud-based solution. A fully functional 14-day trial is available at www.keatext.ai. The software does sentiment analysis. It ranks words by frequency and shows the positive, negative and neutral sentiment proportions using an attractive graphic format. Clicking on any of the circles on the right takes you to a diagram that clusters words that have been used together with the word in question. It does limited word grouping. In Exhibit 9.6 below, I suppose the fact that 'professeur' was in French prevented it being grouped with the similar words at the bottom of the table.

For NPS surveys, you can select the question you want to analyze, and can filter using demographic fields. Excel was used as the input format for this study. The software only works correctly in English, as it cannot display accented characters, at least using Chrome. Overall, Keatext is a nice improvement on word cloud software. It is Natural Language Processing software and it is constantly being improved. In my opinion, the most important next step would be to improve the ability to extract multi-word topics.

## Exhibit 9.6

Keatext - Sift

Most Talked About Topics   overall ∨   [Search]   🏷 Tag

| Topic | Records | | Opinion | | |
|---|---|---|---|---|---|
| cour | 78 | 30.8% | | negative | 3.5% |
| | | | | positive | 15.1% |
| | | | | neutral | 81.4% |
| professeur | 41 | 16.2% | | negative | 2.2% |
| | | | | positive | 28.3% |
| | | | | neutral | 69.6% |
| campus | 28 | 11.1% | | negative | 3.6% |
| | | | | positive | 28.6% |
| | | | | neutral | 67.9% |
| facult | 27 | 10.7% | | negative | 3.4% |
| | | | | positive | 13.8% |
| | | | | neutral | 82.8% |
| niveau | 24 | 9.5% | | negative | 4.2% |
| | | | | positive | 37.5% |
| | | | | neutral | 58.3% |
| enseignement | 23 | 9.1% | | negative | 0% |
| | | | | positive | 40% |
| | | | | neutral | 60% |
| prof (prof, professor) | 22 | 8.7% | | negative | 4.2% |
| | | | | positive | 25% |
| | | | | neutral | 70.8% |

1  2  3  4  5  ⊙

## SurveyTagger

SurveyTagger is no longer being developed as Etuma is concentrating on their enterprise solution, Etuma Feedback Categorizer. (See the additional paragraph on the new software below.) The software is an evolution of earlier software used to manually tag survey results. SurveyTagger tags automatically and works in many languages that use western character sets. Since the authors are Finnish, I suppose they realized they needed to get beyond Finnish to be successful. No matter what the input language, the results are displayed in English, as shown in Exhibit 9.7. There are differences in analysis due to translation. As mentioned, we translated the survey results into English for software testing. The diagram below shows the analysis of the "Why?" question when the input was in English and in French. Note that there are at least some multi-word topics, though not many. Actual survey responses can be shown below the graphs. You can drill down a little by clicking on an individual item.

### Exhibit 9.7

Survey Tagger

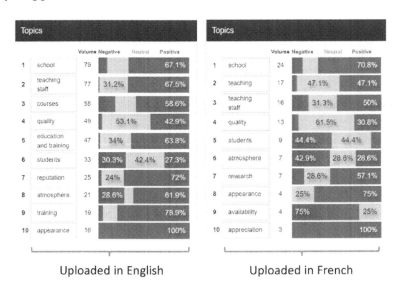

Uploaded in English          Uploaded in French

Etuma Feedback Categorizer
While it is not immediately obvious that it is possible to try out this new software for free, it can be done by sending your file to Etuma. (The software was tested after the business-school project was completed, so has not been included in the results table.) They have taken what they learned from Survey Tagger and applied it to this more sophisticated solution. The software does what it claims, namely categorizes survey feedback. It adds some useful elements to the categorization.

In the first view in Exhibit 9.8, you can see the Promoter / Passive / Detractor NPS status of people who have mentioned each topic. In all views, the issue with single-word topics remains evident, especially compared with the human analysis shown above. The whole subject of the beauty of the campus on the shores of Lake Geneva does not really show up. 'Appearance' is there, but appearance of what?

**Exhibit 9.8**

Etuma feedback categorizer

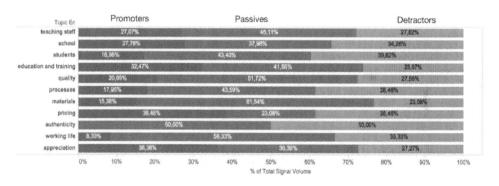

A nice touch in the Feedback Categorizer is the new 'Ambience' view. It provides a sentiment-based graph making it easy to know whether a topic has been mentioned in a positive or negative way.

The same data is used for the word cloud view that is combined with the Ambience bar chart in Exhibit 9.9.

**Exhibit 9.9**

Etuma Ambience view

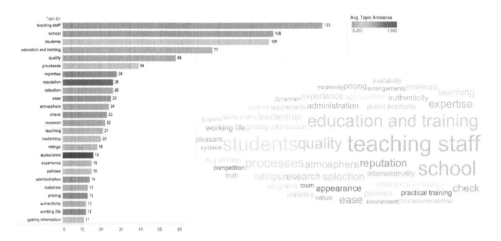

SPSS Text Analysis for Surveys

IBM acquired SPSS a few years ago. SPSS is generally viewed as the premier statistical analysis software. As you might expect, their SPSS Text Analysis for Surveys software is detailed and complete. Perhaps too detailed and too complete for most people, as shown in Exhibit 9.10.

The trial version works in English, is fully functional and can be downloaded from http://www-03.ibm.com/software/products/en/spss-text-analytics-surveys.

SPSS comes with several taxonomies and these are essential to the correct grouping of topics. There was no education taxonomy in the trial version, so the brand image data was used instead. There are lots of options. Their website explains how to drill down into categories and combine them manually. It is possible to export the results into SPSS for statistical analysis and for better graphing capabilities.

Verdict: too detailed for the casual user. Too difficult to get to grips with the software and summarize the actions that need to be taken from a survey.

## Exhibit 9.10

### IBM SPSS

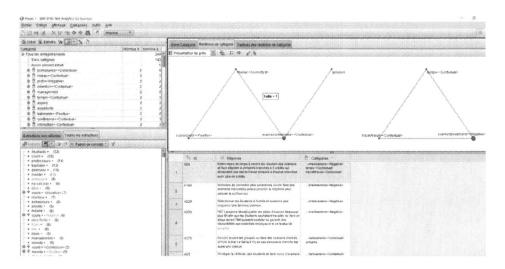

Semantria by Lexalytics

This was the best of three Excel plug-ins at one important task: the identification of multi-word topics. It produces useful multi-word word clouds and works well in French. The word clouds are rather exotic Excel Pivot Charts. As with all Pivot Charts and Pivot Tables, clicking on any element takes you to a new sheet with the corresponding underlying data.

The software performs sentiment analysis and provides a sentiment score. It did a nice job on the "Why?" question and did not do so well with the improvement suggestions. The improvement suggestions varied widely and no software was great at grouping similar multi-word topics together. Humans are much better at this so far.

The screen-captures that are combined in Exhibit 9.11 show the main interface and the clouds for both open-ended questions. The people at Lexalytics have released a version that is specific to survey analysis in late 2016, too late for the study. It currently supports 22 languages.

## Exhibit 9.11

Semantria by Lexalytics – Excel plug-in

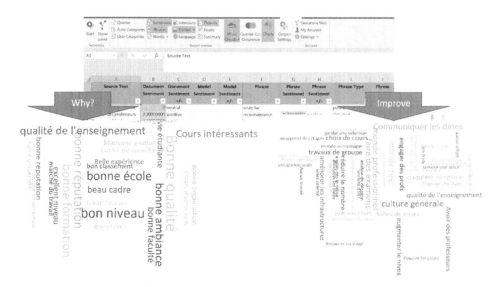

## MeaningCloud

MeaningCloud is a free Excel plug-in available at www.meaningcloud.com. The authors suggest using it for surveys and social media analysis. It does some sentiment analysis and works in French, and of course in English. As supplied, it is quite interesting, but does not classify some responses correctly. By that I mean that some of the positive and negative sentiment categorization is opposite to the sentiments actually expressed.

You are encouraged to build up your own taxonomy. It was clear that if you build a taxonomy for your industry, it should do a good job of correctly categorizing responses. It was not worth investing the necessary time to build an education taxonomy for this single survey.

Exhibit 9.12 is a screen capture. If you intend to do multiple surveys in a narrow domain, you may find it worthwhile to build up a taxonomy and the software will be more useful.

## Exhibit 9.12
Meaning Cloud Excel plug-in

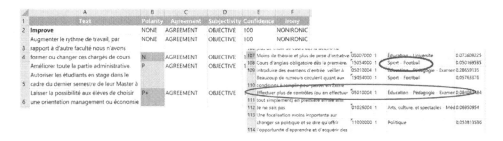

## Text2Data

Text2Data is an Excel plug-in that extracts single and multi-word topics and does sentiment analysis. It does not work in French and the screen capture in Exhibit 9.13 is from the English translation of the survey responses. The problem with the sentiment analysis here is easy to understand from the screenshot. The sentiment words are shown, but not what they refer to. 'Outdated chaotic', OK, but what is outdated and/or chaotic? You have to go back to the individual responses, so the summarization really does not work well. In short, the software was not immediately useful and was not explored in greater depth.

## Exhibit 9.13
Text2Data Excel plug-in

## Robust operational and analytic infrastructure

### Haven OnDemand NPS analytics
The NPS analytics application has been written using the Haven OnDemand cloud-based Application Programming Interfaces (APIs) and is free to use. It can be found in the Solutions menu at www.havenondemand.com. You must register to use it.

The code for the application has been open-sourced on Github at https://github.com/hpe-idol/netpromoter. Haven OnDemand was developed in the software division of Hewlett Packard Enterprise. HPE announced that the software division would be merged with UK company Micro Focus during 2017 and set up as an independent entity, 51% owned by HPE.

In English, Haven OnDemand did the best job of any software investigated, though it did not do as well in French. Since it finished second overall in the study, let's look at it in a bit more detail.

### Haven OnDemand background
Haven OnDemand is a set of cloud-based APIs that can be strung together to create powerful applications. Some are very entertaining. If you search YouTube, you should be able to find a Nerf gun that has been programmed to do facial recognition.

The NPS application uses only IDOL functions. IDOL stands for Intelligent Data Operating Layer and came from Autonomy Inc., which was acquired by HP. IDOL is used for analyzing all types of unstructured data, including video, audio, and of course text. It works to some extent in over 100 languages, including Vogon and Klingon. (Software programmers do not get out much and tend to like science fiction. I can relate to that, based on overnight stints in the computer room while I was still a student) The sentiment analysis API that is used in the NPS application works well in 14 languages.

A very partial list of the APIs is in Exhibit 9.14. Exhibit 9.15 shows what the output looks like.

# Evaluating text analytics software

## Exhibit 9.14

### Haven OnDemand functions – Partial list

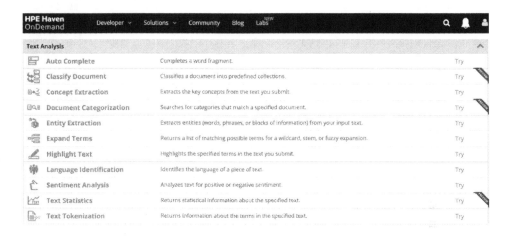

## Exhibit 9.15

### Haven OnDemand – What it looks like

# Robust operational and analytic infrastructure

Distinguishing features
Compared to everything else tested, the Haven OnDemand application did three things best:

- It groups related topics together, even if the words used in the topics are not exact matches.
- It allows you to exclude single-word topics from your results. Assuming you have sufficient data, this works particularly well in English, not so well in French, Italian and Spanish. The Mandarin tester told me it did an OK job there too, though the concept of a single word is different in Mandarin.
- The bar chart presentation is the easiest to understand of any software tested.

Like all other software tested, it is poor at pronoun handling.

Results
Exhibits 9.16 and 9.17 the ones my daughter used to evaluate the software tested for her project. Since Etuma Feedback Categorizer was tested later, it is not included in the table. In principle, it would score lower than Survey Tagger for access, since it cannot be used without assistance in a demo version, and higher for filtering and presentation.

Guess what? Humans win! We can't be replaced (yet). We win because we are still better at understanding how to interpret pronouns and give context to what we read. Note that if your survey needs differ from those of the study, your ranking will differ too.

# Evaluating text analytics software

## Exhibit 9.16

Judging criteria and scores – Scores can be from 1 to 6

|  | Access, read and extract | Frequency of topics | Recognize sentiment | Summarize | Filtering (refine report) | Present |
|---|---|---|---|---|---|---|
| Humans | 5 | 3 | 6 | 4 | 1 | 6 |
| DataCracker | 2 | 2 | 1 | 1 | 2 | 2 |
| WordyUp | 2 | 1 | 1 | 2 | 1 | 2 |
| Wordclouds.com | 2 | 2 | 1 | 1 | 1 | 2 |
| Sift Keatext | 2 | 4 | 5 | 3 | 4 | 4 |
| SurveyTagger | 2 | 6 | 5 | 3 | 2 | 4 |
| SPSS | 3 | 5 | 6 | 1 | 1 | 2 |
| Lexalytics | 3 | 5 | 6 | 4 | 2 | 3 |
| MeaningCloud | 1 | 2 | 4 | 1 | 1 | 1 |
| Text2Data | 1 | 2 | 3 | 2 | 1 | 1 |
| Haven OnDemand | 2 | 3 | 5 | 5 | 4 | 5 |

## Exhibit 9.17

Final results

| | Final Score | Place |
|---|---|---|
| Humans | 25 | 1 |
| DataCracker | 10 | |
| WordyUp | 9 | |
| Wordclouds.com | 9 | |
| Sift Keatext | 22 | 4 |
| SurveyTagger | 22 | 4 |
| SPSS | 18 | |
| Lexalytics | 23 | 3 |
| MeaningCloud | 10 | |
| Text2Data | 10 | |
| Haven OnDemand | 24 | 2 |

"Can you believe how cute they are when they win?"

Haven OnDemand

"I'm seriously considering keeping one."

Lexalytics

# 9.5 A commercial software example

Text analysis software is in constant evolution. A New Zealand-based startup, Thematic (www.getthematic.com), is a great example of a company that has developed new algorithms for Natural Language Processing and has started to produce exceptional results. The CEO and founder, Alyona Medelyan, did her doctorate in keyword extraction, and seems to have achieved a breakthrough in the identification of multi-word topics and concept groups, or 'Themes'. There is no free trial version, so Thematic did not fit the criteria for the university student survey. Nonetheless, they provided an analysis without charge. For their own purposes, they have anonymized the results, changed the name of the university to Hogwarts and use it on their customer portal to demonstrate the software.

**Exhibit 9.18**

Thematic – Top level

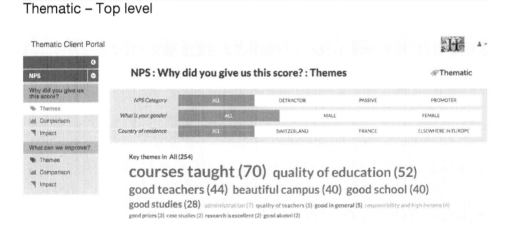

Exhibit 9.18 shows what the top-level output looks like. The grouping of similar words into multi-word themes is particularly well done. Note the list on the left that allows you to choose which of the two open NPS questions you analyze. Mousing over a theme reveals sub-themes and mousing over

# A commercial software example

a sub-theme reveals representative comments. The three horizontal bars at the top allow drill-down analysis. The first bar lets you select the NPS category, and the other two correspond to two demographics questions asked in the survey. The demographic choices are available in each view, and make it easy to compare answers from men to those from women, for example.

The results are the best I have seen from any software solution tried so far, by a clear margin. The only significant improvement I can see as possible is to have it work natively in languages other than English. In its current version, anything that is not in English is automatically translated before analysis.

Selecting the 'Comparison' menu choice reveals 'Base themes' themes as shown in Exhibit 9.19. Clicking on each shows sub-themes, as seen for 'beautiful campus' in this example.

## Exhibit 9.19

Thematic – Answers to the 'Why?' question

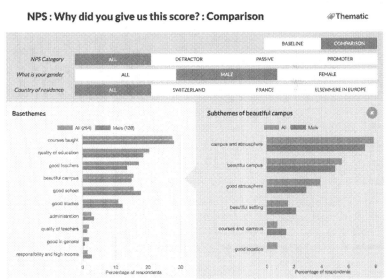

# Robust operational and analytic infrastructure

And Exhibit 9.20 below shows an analysis of the impact of any individual item on the overall score. In this example, I clicked on the negative 'Administration' theme and looked at the difference in scores between students living normally in Switzerland, compared to the average. I also used the 'baseline' and 'comparison' feature to compare what students normally resident in Switzerland said about the beauty of the campus, compared to students who normally live in France. See Exhibit 9.21. The Swiss seem blasé about the spectacular view of Lake Geneva and the Alps.

## Exhibit 9.20

Thematic – Impact of any 'Base theme' on the score

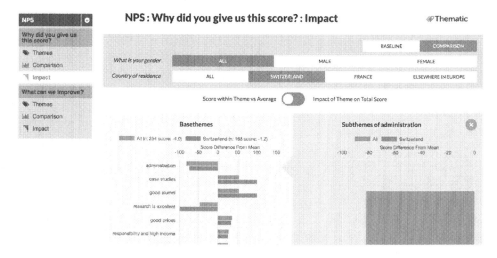

## Exhibit 9.21

Comparison of French and Swiss student views on the campus

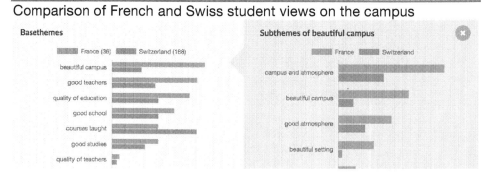

# A commercial software example

## The technology

Exhibit 9.22 is a diagram from their website that explains how Thematic works. The 'refinements' step is manual and is optional. The intellectual property was designed by the founder, using ideas from her Ph.D. thesis on keyword extraction, and the latest advances in Deep Learning.

## Exhibit 9.22

Thematic – How it works

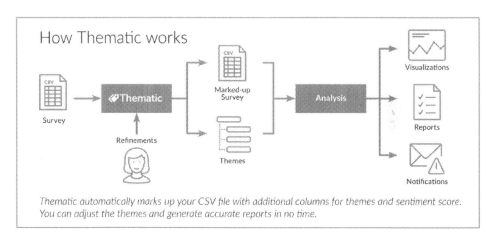

Thematic automatically marks up your CSV file with additional columns for themes and sentiment score. You can adjust the themes and generate accurate reports in no time.

## Conclusion

Like all other software, Thematic is not perfect, and will continue to improve. Humans continue to understand language better than machines. Thematic and other solutions should be used for initial screening and to reduce human bias. A combination of human and software analysis will give the best results. Note in passing that the author has no involvement or financial interest in Thematic. The software has simply been used to illustrate best practice at the time of writing.

## 9.6 Human-machine collaboration

"You swapped the queen for a pawn??!?"

"Did not!"

"So did!"

"It looked like a bishop."

"How much are you worth as scrap?"

"More than you."

IBM's Deep Blue software famously defeated Gary Kasparov in 1996. Far from being bitter about it, Kasparov became a promoter of human-machine collaboration. His breakthrough came when he observed what happened in some chess tournaments where players were allowed consult even the simplest chess applications. Here is what he said about the subject in the New York Review of Books:

> *"Having a computer program available during play was as disturbing as it was exciting. The machine doesn't care about style or patterns or hundreds of years of established theory," he added. "It is entirely free of prejudice and doctrine, and this has contributed to the development of players who are almost as free of dogma as the machines with which they train. Increasingly, a move isn't good or bad because it looks that way or because it hasn't been*

*done that way before. It's simply good if it works and bad if it doesn't. Although we still require a strong measure of intuition and logic to play well, humans today are starting to play more like computers."*

Collaborative future

I believe some of the language understanding problems I have identified are simply too difficult to solve. They don't make software useless. They simply mean that humans should consult software, take its suggestions into account, use it as a bias checker, then draw their own conclusions, deciding their own chess moves.

## 9.7 Learning check

Decide whether each of the following statements is true or false:

- Customer Experience is clearly a part of brand marketing and the customer experience leader should always report to the Marketing leader.
- Humans are currently the best single solution for evaluating and prioritizing verbatim responses to surveys.

# 10. Employee/Team environment focused on loyalty

## 10.1 Do happy employees matter?

"Welcome, dear customer. We are all so happy here."

Contrary to popular wisdom, happy employees are not terribly important to customers. My research shows that employee happiness contributes about 0.9% of customer happiness. This does vary by industry.

Source of data
I compared American Customer Satisfaction Index data with Glassdoor.com employee ratings for 336 large companies that sell to US consumers. The research has been described in detail in the companion book on B2B customer experience strategy. Using linear regression, just 0.9% of the variability in customer satisfaction is due to employee satisfaction. For the stats experts, the number rises to just 1.0% with quadratic regression.

Reasons for the surprise
There are a number of reasons the link between end customer and employee happiness is not as high as you might expect:

- First and foremost, a happy employee is not necessarily an engaged employee. A person can be happy with their short commute to work, their pay, and the free food in the company restaurant. None of these involves doing anything positive for customers. Engagement is a more complex concept, with no standard definition. However, every study I have seen shows a positive relationship between employee engagement and a range of things, such as financial results and customer satisfaction.

- Many brands do not actually interact directly with customers at all. This is the case for franchise businesses. The company grants a right to use a brand in a geographical area to a franchise operator and the franchisee is the one who interacts with the end customer. Even the largest corporations that deliver physical goods do this to an extent. Almost none cover every country in the world themselves, depending on local third-parties to cover their gaps. The happiness of the employees who have no interaction with the end customer is of course invisible to them and has no impact on their NPS scores received from those end customers. The parent companies should be more concerned with the happiness of franchisees. There is no easily-available public data on franchise operator NPS.

- There are web-only brands where you are unlikely to come into contact with a human. Amazon is a company with a great ASCI score of 86, and a mediocre Glassdoor score of 3.4.

- Some brands have monopolies and can afford to treat customers poorly. This seems notably to be the case for cable TV companies and Internet Service Providers. Their customer and employee satisfaction scores seem to be opposites. Who would have thought it possible? Happy employees and unhappy customers.

## There may be sectors where it matters a lot

My research suggests there are high-touch industries where employee engagement makes a difference to customers. There were 16 supermarket chains in my study, and the correlation between ACSI scores and employee happiness was a very-high 0.630. Specialty retail stores and investor-owned utilities were also well-represented and had correlations around 0.4. Hotels had the highest correlation of all, with 0.857 for the ten chains represented. However, those companies include hotels operated by franchisees, rather than employees of the parent company, and ten is not a great population for calculating correlation coefficients. Bearing this in mind, I nevertheless selected 117 of the 336 companies covered as 'High touch', and found that variations in employee satisfaction explain 3.4% of the variations in customer satisfaction, using linear regression, and 6.1% using quadratic regression.

## Think about it

If you were to assemble a team of people and ask them to brainstorm potential factors that affect customer happiness and loyalty, I believe you would come up with a long list. Employee satisfaction would probably make the list, but I doubt it would be in the top five. Things like the reliability of your products would be higher up on the list. It is only when the question is asked in isolation that people say employee satisfaction is the most critical factor. It is a case of an intuitive reaction, rather than a rational one. It would be tempting to believe that employee satisfaction is a hygiene factor, meaning that unhappy employees do indeed have a negative effect on customers, and that there is a diminishing rate or return on improving happiness, making no difference at all above a certain point. However, the ACSI analysis does not support that theory either. The relationship is close to linear at the cross-industry level.

# 10.2 eNPS

Most medium and large companies, NGOs and public sector organizations measure employee happiness in a structured way, on a regular basis. The purpose of such research is usually to help executives to understand what the general employee population would like them to improve. The CEO also gets to find out what improvements the executives would like to see. Almost everyone uses excessively complex survey methods that take too long and provide limited information about improvement suggestions. Applying the Net Promoter System solves these problems. Employee Net Promoter Scores are the answers to the question: "How likely are you to recommend our company as a place to work?"

How not to measure employee satisfaction
Most companies that measure employee satisfaction do so once a year. Data collection is a significant exercise and a typical survey has about 80 questions. Analysis is often done by a third party. Results are usually available four to eight weeks after the survey period ends. Companies may further delay publication for various real or imagined reasons, such as not wanting them to compete for attention with quarterly earnings messages. Sub-scores are calculated for areas like employee engagement, or compensation & benefits. There may or may not be open questions with free text input. To use an old saying, the result of such surveys is far too much data and far too little information. Let's suppose your employee engagement questions score lower than last year, and lower than the average for your industry. Since you only have numbers, you don't know why it happened. The usual first phase is one of denial, "Well, we had a major management change right in the middle of the survey period, so the change is understandable. Let's wait until next year to see if we need to act." If you can get through that sort of reaction, the next phase is one of focus groups. You may have collected data from 10,000 people, but the decisions about what to do are given to a group of ten people, for example. You could really have started there, skipping the survey, if you think that is a good approach.

Benchmarks

There are no recognized benchmark suppliers for eNPS. The Mayflower group in the USA and the RACER group in Germany have set up agreements among member companies to share employee survey data. The IT Survey Group (ITSG) is a recognized source of non-eNPS employee survey benchmark data for the IT industry. Member companies agree to ask 60 survey questions in exactly the same format, and using the same rating scale. They then use the average ratings as a norm for their own scores. There are no verbatim questions in the ITSG data set, so there is no information on what the average IT industry employee would like his or her company to improve.

The 20 companies in Exhibit 10.1 are the ITSG members at the time of writing. They all use the long-format surveys ITSG membership requires. At HP, we took the comparison with ITSG numbers seriously. We just did not directly know what to do.

**Exhibit 10.1**

ITSG members

## Employee/Team environment focused on loyalty

Let's make it a lot simpler

The Net Promoter System presents an obvious way of doing simpler surveys. Simply ask employees whether they would recommend your company, why that is, and what you should improve. You already have all the demographic information you need about them, so analysis should be easy. Yes, the demographics matter a lot. Men and women tend to give radically different answers, for example. Happiness tends to decrease with increasing length of service.

No matter what the demographic group, the trend is more important than the absolute number. This brings us to another advantage of the eNPS method. I recommend sampling one-sixth of your population every month, sending new survey requests each and every day. The great advantage this brings is that you will be able to see the effect of different things happening in your company, such as earnings announcements, new product announcements, executive arrivals or departures, and even external factors such as a stock market crash or an election.

Follow the NPS framework

The NPS framework works for eNPS as well. Employee feedback is normally anonymous. Typically, a manager will only receive a report if at least eight of her employees have provided feedback. The Inner Loop then takes place at the level of each team. The Outer Loop addresses company-wide improvements. Regular Huddles are the correct way to drive progress and ensure interlock between inner and outer loops.

Indirect advantage

On top of simplicity, and the ability to do continuous monitoring, there is an indirect benefit. All employees will become familiar with NPS. They will easily understand that you are asking customers and employees the same questions and follow the same improvement process. Of course, if you take no visible action on the employee feedback, it will be harder to persuade employees that you are indeed acting on customer feedback. You need to do both.

Cultural differences matter a lot in traditional employee surveys less in eNPS

While cultural differences matter somewhat in customer surveys, they seem to matter a lot more in employee surveys. CEB (www.cebglobal.com) has published Exhibit 10.2 that emphasizes the point.

**Exhibit 10.2**

CEB self-rating results by country

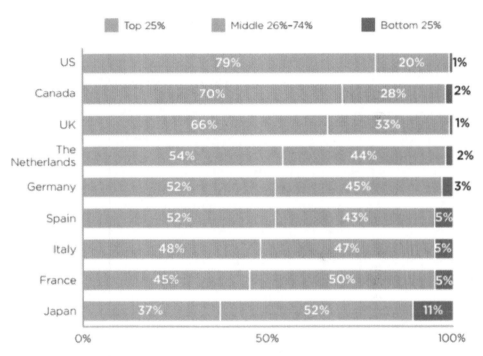

In short, unrealistic self-perceptions of performance are common. These differences are greater than those found between countries for customer surveys. Personally, I find the table surprising. North Americans use 'curve grading' in their schools. Curve grading means that a fixed proportion of a class gets an 'A' grade, a 'B' and so on, no matter what the objective level of the class is. Most Americans therefore grow up having a realistic view of how they compare to others in the classroom. Apparently, this knowledge is discarded when they enter the world of work. Curve grading is rare in the other countries on the list. Could these facts be related? I could speculate, but don't really see how they could be.

## An additional communication challenge

We have seen that you should not compare countries to each other in your reporting. A fair way of reporting on countries would be to show only the trends, not the absolute numbers. Just leave the numbers off the y-axis in your graphs. There is an additional communication challenge with eNPS. I have generally seen eNPS scores that are about 20 points lower than the customer scores for a given business. What that means is that eNPS scores are far more likely to be negative numbers than are customer scores.

As previously advised, if your first report on a topic only contains bright red negative numbers, your audience will intuitively deny the reality of your report and ignore it. Rather than perverting the system by (say) adding 20 points to all the numbers to 'normalize' them, I suggest devoting the first report entirely to the improvement suggestions, and the answers to the Why question. You can supply the positive or negative eNPS trend numbers from the second report on, without necessarily providing the absolute scores at all. You may like to believe your audience will have a rational response to a set of negative numbers, but they will not. Intuition rules. Deal with it.

## Conclusion

Use eNPS as your primary ongoing survey methodology, and execute it continuously. If you (mistakenly, I believe) think you get value from participating in a benchmark consortium, continue to do that huge survey for a year or two, comparing the actions you take from each survey type. I am confident you will discard the consortium survey, particularly as it does not give you direct insight on the performance of any individual competitor. If you genuinely want to improve things for your employees, just ask them what to do, then do it. The Employee Net Promoter System and Score are the most efficient and effective way of doing so.

# 10.3 ceNPS

W e have talked about asking customers what to improve, and improving it. We have mentioned the same approach for employees. I now want to introduce a hybrid concept: ask employees what to improve for customers. Let's call it Customer-Employee NPS, or ceNPS.

Why should the customer be the only source of customer knowledge? Customers are the best possible source for information about what they would like to see improved. As to how to improve it, well, they leave that up to you. Your employees have a different perspective. Most are aware of things that could be made better for customers. Many also have precise ideas about exactly how to do so. I therefore suggest testing the following survey with your employees to see what value it provides:

1. How likely are our customers to recommend our company?
2. Why?
3. What should we improve for customers and how?

Use the same techniques as for customer research to prioritize the input. I don't see why this would not work in all industries, bearing in mind that 'customer' means the direct customer of the company, which could be a retailer that sells onwards to end customers.

Compare with customer feedback
In a rational universe, there will be at least some overlap between customer feedback and employee views on what customers need. Compare the top five suggestions on both lists. Items that come up high on both lists are ideal; the customer's expression of the need will match employee suggestions on how to implement the improvement.

## Employee/Team environment focused on loyalty

Employees will have different ideas

Employees may have insights in areas that would not naturally occur to customers. One example that springs to mind happened shortly after HP set up a centralized pre-sales group in Bucharest, Romania. When the new operation started up, it would be fair to say that the people were quite passive, just doing what was asked. Sales people and resellers asked them to provide price quotations to customers, and they did that work well. Then the team supporting the Benelux noticed something. As negotiation cycles continued, sales people removed things from orders to meet a customer price point. Notably, offers for servers and storage that started with round-the-clock support services were often reduced to a cheaper business-hours-only proposal.

The Benelux team in Bucharest decided to systematically give the customers two proposals: one exactly as requested, and one with the service levels they believed the customers really needed, at a higher price. The initiative was a great success, with about half the customers taking the more appropriate service proposal at the higher price. For customers who accepted, it completely eliminated the situations where they would call during a weekend to be told that their contract did not cover the repair. A customer would never have thought of this double-proposal idea.

Employees should lead the implementation of their own ideas

Unless you have an excellent reason for not doing so, the person who made the suggestion should always lead implementation. Letting anyone else lead eliminates a career development opportunity and allows one aspect of human nature to creep into the picture: rejection of other people's ideas. Just as the golden rule of project planning is "Those who implement must do the planning", the golden rule of ideas, is that the idea generator must drive the implementation. Yes, it is true that really creative people are usually awful at implementation, and that will be their career development opportunity.

Include your subcontractors and partners

If you use resellers and subcontractors, they should be included in your improvement culture too. Simply follow the same approach as for employees. I know of no example of any company doing this, and am sure the reaction will be positive. It is to be expected that your partners will have privileged relationships with some of your end customers. You need to learn from them.

# 10.4 Employee development

M any companies have employee training and development processes. Here is how the Net Promoter System should be included in three common types of training programs.

Graduate development programs
Most large companies have formal programs to hire and develop graduates from targeted business schools. Company representatives have stands at university recruitment days. They also proactively contact students in particular classes, trying to position the company as an attractive place to work. Once of the common graduate benefits is a formal training program for new hires, along with guaranteed minimum salary increases for the first year or two. One the one hand, these new hires may rise quickly in the organization. On the other hand, they are relatively unlikely to stay for more than a couple of years.

The customer experience leader needs to contact the leader of the graduate program and supply the NPS training content without being asked. If there is a welcome pack or website for new people, your customer listening and improvement process needs to be part of it. Be open about what customers want the company to improve. I don't see a reason to directly involve new hires in the improvement work. They simply need to understand what the overall process looks like.

Top Talent programs, Fast Track programs
HR evaluation processes are used to identify 'top talent' in many companies. These are the people who have high formal performance ratings and who have been subjectively identified as having strong growth potential. (If you think you work for a company that has abandoned formal performance reviews, you are kidding yourself. They still exist, and have simply been given a different name. There is always some fact-based

process for distributing money from the annual salary increase and bonus pools.)

I have been involved in several such programs, and it has always surprised me how difficult the organizers find it to develop the curriculum, when it is done internally. This is a great opportunity. I have found them receptive to proposals to deliver customer-centric content myself. The most common proposal I have made in recent years is to start by explaining the Net Promoter System and the latest competitive benchmark results. The participants are then invited to brainstorm and develop improvement initiatives that they then manage while they participate in the program. The last time I did this at HP, I was given a full day of the three-day opening session.

## Individual development plans
Most medium and large companies require managers to agree job plans and development plans with each of their employees. It may be counterproductive to require all managers to include a customer-centric objective, as most will be meaningless. A better approach is to write to managers who are about to start working on the development plans. Provide them with a list of the improvements customers and partners are requesting, and suggest which ones might be appropriate for a specific manager's people. Offer to support the formal documentation and implementation of relevant projects.

## NPS professional certification
There are not many sources of professional certification for the Net Promoter System. Bain provides customized training for individual clients, though no recognized certification. Satmetrix is the only official source of certification for your NPS professionals. Official means recognized as such by the co-inventors, Fred Reichheld, Bain and Satmetrix. The current certification is for what Satmetrix calls NPS2. They position it as NPS for the internet age and have improved the definitions of the feedback and improvement processes to take social media and such factors into account. Personally, I find the new training more complex than it needs to be. You can find introductory videos and decide for yourself at

www.netpromoter.com. Medallia also provides NPS training, though it concentrates on aspects that support the use of Medallia software. Not quite ideal.

## Conclusion

Inclusion of the Net Promoter System in company hiring and development programs will not happen spontaneously. The customer experience leader needs to find out what development programs exist, and get involved at the appropriate time. Some of the timing is predictable, such as when graduates are likely to join, and when HR requires all development plans to be submitted in Workday, or whatever management tool your company uses. Be proactive.

## 10.5 Learning check

Decide whether each of these statements is true or false:

- Happy employees are the single most important customer satisfaction predictor in most businesses.
- The Net Promoter System work just as well as an employee experience improvement process as it does for customers.
- Satmetrix is the only official provider of Net Promoter professional certification.

# 11.   Sustained leadership commitment

# 11.1 Do you have it?

The questions addressed here are about the true level of commitment of your leadership to improving customer loyalty and mid-term financial performance. We will cover how to tell whether you have the commitment already, and what you should do if not.

Are your leaders already committed?
Don't start by making assumptions. Do your research. If you work for a public company, download and read your annual report. Read your latest earnings announcement. If your company does a quarterly earnings conference call with financial and industry analysts, try to join the call. Download the slides used for the call and inspect them. Assuming your company strategy is stated somewhere in all this material, what is it? Are customers mentioned among the top few priorities? While it could have changed by the time you read this, many consider Apple to be customer-centric, but Apple does not mention customer experience in any of these documents at the time of writing. They are in fact a product-centric company. This does not mean they don't care about customers at all; far

from it. In a product-centric company, work on customer experience simply has to be positioned as supporting product growth.

## Prompted versus unprompted support

Reading your CEO and senior leaders' all-employee emails is close to reading what psychologists call an unprompted response. Unprompted reactions to questions tell you what a person really feels. The prompted reactions of a senior executive bring political correctness into play. Think about what would happen were you to ask these questions in the Q&A section, after your CEO has spoken to all employees. Accept for a moment that all three start with "You have told us your top five priorities, but you have not mentioned..."

- "...that only 15% of the people managers in the company are women while we represent 40% of the workforce. Do you not think this is important?"
- "...that most other companies around here give paid time off for employees to do volunteer work in the community. How much do local communities matter to our company?
- "...our customers as a priority. Where are customers on your list?"

Faced with such prompting, the CEO is forced to reply that he/she is launching a major initiative to double the number of female managers, that we can look forward to an announcement about volunteering, and that customers are central to everything we do, so should not be mentioned separately, or something similar. None of these responses change the reality of the top priorities: the list the CEO gives without prompting. If customer experience is not on your company's formal priority short list, you can change it over time, with patience and persistence.

## Leaders' job history may work against you

If your company hires leaders from outside, it can pose particularly difficult problems. After all, the executive who has been poached is naturally convinced that he or she has been hired for their beliefs, knowledge and results, as well as the business practices and results of the former employer. If her former company had better results than yours, and did not use the Net

# Do you have it?

Promoter System, it is unlikely that she can easily be persuaded to adopt it. She is more likely to propose that NPS be abandoned in favor of whatever she is used to. This is where your CFO should help, assuming you have jointly proven the financial effect of NPS trends for your company. (This won't work if the new executive is the CFO, of course.) If the executive's former company is one of your competitors, NPS should be positioned as a way you are going to catch up and overtake them. That position is hard to argue with, as most executives understand that you can never overtake a competitor by copying exactly what they have been doing.

Do your leaders spend much time with customers?
According to Bain research shown in Exhibit 11.1, the larger the company, the more time leaders spend on internal meetings, rather than directly with customers. They know this and they hate it.

## Exhibit 11.1

Executive time spent with customers by size of company

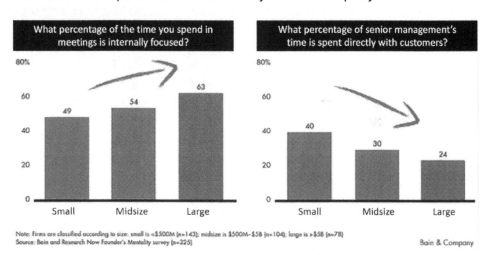

Note: Firms are classified according to size: small is <$500M (n=143); midsize is $500M–$5B (n=104); large is >$5B (n=78)
Source: Bain and Research Now Founder's Mentality survey (n=325)

Bain & Company

Ask your senior managers how much of their time they spend with customers and how much they would like to spend. If they currently devote more than the proportions below to customers, you can consider them to be committed. All of this has a perverse benefit for the customer experience leader in a large company. If you can come up with simple proposals that let leaders spend more time with customers, and with minimal effort on their part, you will win.

## Check your Intranet

Now you know what is being said publicly. Are the public statements about customers backed up by the internal priority list? What has the CEO said in his or her latest email message to all employees? Assuming you have an intranet, go to the home page of each member of the corporate leadership team. Look for their lists of priorities for their teams. Are customers mentioned? If you work for a large company, look one layer down. What do you see? I suggest making a table with all the priority lists and discussing it with your leadership team.

## Do the actions match the words?

Now you know what your leaders are saying. Time to inspect what they are doing. Start internally. Does your company hold events for sales teams? Do customers or partners attend and speak at these events? If you have effective monopolies in some product areas, what has been your approach to pricing? Do you put prices up each and every year, as some notorious pharmaceutical companies have been seen to do? If you are in software and perform license audits on customers, is it done by a helpful operations person or an aggressive lawyer? What is your supply chain team's attitude to their operational metrics like level of fill and delivery to customer commit dates? Is there evidence that both the standard and the performance have been steadily improving over time, or does cost reduction seem to compromise that?

## Price gouging — a particularly insidious move

As this is written, the New York Attorney General has launched an investigation into Mylan Pharmaceuticals, the maker of EpiPens. An EpiPen is used to provide life-saving injections to people in anaphylactic shock, due to allergies. The reason for the investigation is that Mylan have had a monopoly on the product and have increased its price in the USA by 471% since acquiring it in 2007. The CEO's initial public attitude to this seems to be "Hey… I am just running a business here."

# Do you have it?

Daniel Kahneman has written about price fairness and the consequences of unfair pricing in Thinking, Fast and Slow. He gives examples of a hardware store that puts up the prices of snow shovels by a third during a storm, and of an employer putting down the salary of an existing employee due to competition. Very few people consider these practices to be fair. So what? So… he goes on to cover the revenge customers are prepared to take when they see an unfair practice. Indeed, not only will customers take revenge, many other people who are not customers will happily join in to punish the unfair practice and they will all feel great about it. This is what is currently happening with Mylan. Go to their website at www.mylan.com. It purports to show how caring they are. The actions do not seem to match the words.

Corporate goals can conflict with each other

In larger companies, each corporate function can have goals that seem perfectly sensible in isolation, but conflict with each other. I remember one of these situations arising when I was in the HP office in the center of Prague. A bank across the road had a guaranteed 30-minute intervention time for their systems. We held spare parts in our building for them. The local team were unpleasantly surprised by the results of the corporate Real

## Sustained leadership commitment

Estate team's cost reduction goals. We had to leave the expensive office downtown and move to a cheaper location, making it impossible to honor the service time guarantee with existing processes.

A similar exercise led to a proposal to close a remote parts stocking location in the east of Russia. The next-closest office was over a thousand miles away. Our response time guarantee to a local oil company was at risk. Unfortunately, we had to find more expensive solutions for servicing the customers while still allowing the Real Estate team to make their goals. If you work at a company that needs to reduce costs, try hard to ensure that each cost goal that could impact a customer is accompanied by an appropriate customer-centric operational metric.

## 11.2 How to get it

Most leaders have a detailed understanding of the area they are responsible for. The majority do not have as detailed an understanding of what they need to improve for customers. This is where the Net Promoter System comes in. If you lead Customer Experience, this should be your main objective. At HP, I made it my business to propose customer-centric priorities to each of the other leadership team members as they went through their annual strategy cycles. At least some of these made it to their formal priority lists. I admit going through a 'name and shame' cycle with screen captures of Intranet sites that listed each leader's priorities. I also supplied suggestions to the people who put those intranet sites together.

### Short versus medium-term
Customers take time to notice and provide feedback on improved customer experience. Improvement actions you take today may take 6 to 18 months to produce a measurable difference in competitive NPS benchmarks. In the meantime, your leaders may have pressure to produce revenue and cost numbers each quarter that cause them to do things that negatively impact customers. This is the one area where there is no real solution. Almost nothing you do in customer experience this week can impact your company results this fiscal quarter. Many other functions have the same challenges, notably Marketing.

### Trying to get leaders to act on facts, not intuition
As my own team published the quarterly competitive NPS benchmarks, I asked to be on the management team agenda for each business and function. The purpose was to review results and priorities. Without exception, the teams were highly engaged. There is somewhat of an art to such presentations, as it is all too easy to show up for a 45-minute presentation slot with 50 slides. Try to prepare the discussion with one slide per 7 to 10 minutes of discussion. You can add backup slides for distribution. The

audience should be at least as interested in your insights about competitors' trends as about your own.

Facing reality — leaders are still going to act first on the basis of intuition and emotion
Feed the intuition. Use emotion. Start your presentations, discussions, speeches and emails using an appropriate emotional appeal to your audience's intuition. Dan Ariely refers to closeness, vividness and the 'drop-in-the-bucket' effect in The Upside of Irrationality.

- *Closeness* is both physical and psychological. If you happen to be in New Zealand, start with an example of a problem faced by a specific local customer. Do not start by talking about a customer in India. Pick a problem your audience can identify with from their everyday lives, even if you believe it is not the most important problem. Think about using long queues for something, the prized Christmas toy being perpetually out of stock at the local store, or perhaps an error in a credit card charge. The problem does not have to be exactly the same as the one on the 'Top 5 customer problem' list; just close enough for your audience to relate to it personally,
- *Vividness* is about including emotion in the way you tell the story. Let's suppose your customers are complaining about delivery errors. Your story could be about how you ordered the latest popular children's toy online for your nine-year-old daughter. You were delighted when the box showed up the day before her birthday, gift-wrapped like you asked. Then tell the audience how your daughter cried when she opened the box and the wrong toy was inside, instead of the long-promised gift.
- *Drop-in-the-bucket* is about whether the people in the audience feel that it is within their individual power to make a difference. If they feel they could work hard on something that would take a long time and make a marginal difference, they will lose interest. If you are discussing a big and difficult problem, you should represent the problem you are addressing in terms of named individuals who work for local customers. At least the audience will feel a desire to help their local 'drops in the bucket'. It is far more effective to sub-divide

a problem into smaller components that provide benefits in the short term. If you are showing that a competitor has a clear lead in three areas, pick one (or a subset of one) that the audience you are addressing can recognize and address themselves. This of course means changing what you say and write, adjusting it to each new audience.

# 11.3 Involving leaders

When Robert Youngjohns was head of Microsoft North America, he used to do something I admire. He held an 'Open hour' for customers about once a month. What this meant was that all customers knew they could dial in to a conference call line and talk to Robert. Since there was no practical limit to the number of people who could join, customers could also hear and dialog with each other. If you copy that, your executive needs to have a reasonably complete grasp of the business and current known issues, and have the self-confidence necessary to say, "I don't know, and will find out" when necessary.

Executive sponsor programs

A practical way of letting senior people spend more time with customers is to implement an executive sponsor program. The role of the sponsor is to improve the overall relationship between your company and the customer or customers to which they are assigned. You should start by agreeing assignments to a single customer each. Ideally, the assignments should correspond to each executive's areas of personal interest. Assigning them to former employers also works, provided they separated on good terms.

It is hard for executives to say no to the program, but not all will actually become active. It can be hard at the customer end too, as other companies may be trying to get time with the same contacts. Somehow, your program has to be different or better than your competitors', or you just won't get the engagement you require. Note that sponsors should never start off by participating in sales discussions about a current deal. That would destroy their relationship-centric credibility.

Listen to calls

Please note the plural in "calls". It is a good idea to let senior people listen to multiple calls in your service center. Once they understand the agents' work, you can let them take a call, supporting them in the same way you would support a new call center agent. If executives listen to calls, it is important to select the calls at random. If they only listen to your best-performing agent, they will have a biased view of the work. If your executives do not listen to enough calls, or just do it once, for a few hours, they will walk away believing that what they have heard is entirely representative of customer views. This means that the customer experience leader needs to do an excellent job of positioning the service center work as a hygiene factor, and needs to remind the executive that most customers do not call the service center. Unfortunately, many large companies outsource service center work for cost reasons, making executive participation difficult to arrange.

## 11.4 Learning check

Decide whether each of these statements is true or false:

- To be most persuasive, customer experience leaders should usually start their presentations with a story about a single customer, a quote from a customer executive, or a single emotionally-charged statement.
- Senior leaders who participate in a company's Executive Sponsor program should have no experience in the client's industry. Customers will welcome their outside views.

# 12.　Where do I start?

# 12.1 Assessing your current state

Y ou almost certainly have something in place today. Getting a free, basic, objective view of how good it is is not all that difficult. Take the free Bain assessment that you will find close to the top of the www.netpromotersystem.com web page. It is hosted by Qualtrics, and you should answer at the level of an individual business in a large company with multiple businesses. When you take the survey, you receive a color-coded assessment of your progress in each of the five areas of the NPS framework. What follows are some screen captures made while I completed an assessment for a client company. It kicks off with Exhibits 12.1 and 12.2.

## Exhibit 12.1

Bain self-assessment

For what type of interactions are you completing the survey: Consumer (B2C) or Channel/Customer (B2B)? Please choose only one, as the way you answer the questions would likely be different for B2C and B2B. If you would like, you can complete the survey multiple times for different aspects of your business.

> Consumer (B2C)

> Channel/Customer (B2B)

How strongly do you agree:
"We have accurately identified and surveyed influencers vs. decision makers at our B2B customers/accounts?"

> Strongly disagree

> Disagree more than agree

> Agree more than disagree

> Strongly agree

215

You are then asked about the size of the business, number of customers, and time since NPS was introduced. The following question takes the general form of an NPS "Why?" question.

## Exhibit 12.2

Bain self-assessment – Success rating

How successful has NPS been at helping you improve your business/organization?

Not at all successful                                                Completely successful

| 0 | 1 | 2 | 3 | 4 | 5 | 6 | 7 | **8** | 9 | 10 |

Why?

> We are quite far from having implemented the main suggestions customers have given us. Constant management changes and merger integrations make it difficult to keep management focus. The CEO was passionate about the subject five years ago, but has other priorities now.

You are then asked what types of NPS research you do, from a list of three: competitive benchmarks, relationship, and transaction surveys. This is followed by questions about each survey type:

- Competitive: the score, the trend, and whether you use the results for improvement purposes.
- Relationship: the score, trend, number of questions, and whether you have precautions in place to avoid over-surveying.
- Event surveys are a bit more problematic in that you can only provide input for a single transactional survey. I suggest using whichever survey gives you the most volume. The questions are about the score, trend, response rate and number of questions. You can answer "Don't know" for the response rate if necessary.

Then come the core questions about perceptions of the system, effectiveness of different aspects, and leadership support. Exhibit 12.3 is a partial list.

## Exhibit 12.3

Bain self-assessment – Perception of the system

| | Strongly disagree | Disagree more than agree | Agree more than disagree | Strongly agree | N/A |
|---|---|---|---|---|---|
| Our most senior executives participate actively in the Net Promoter System (e.g. via regularly reviewing verbatim data, calling customers, visiting sites, allocating sufficient resources, training etc.) | ○ | ○ | ● | ○ | ○ |
| 'Voice of the customer' and 'impact on NPS' are significant inputs to major strategy and investment decisions, on par with other key operational /financial KPIs. | ○ | ○ | ● | ○ | ○ |
| We systematically identify detailed root causes that create Promoters and Detractors. | ○ | ○ | ○ | ● | ○ |
| Our CFO has certified our customer lifetime value calculations for Promoters, Passives and Detractors. | ● | ○ | ○ | ○ | ○ |

## Exhibit 12.4

Bain self-assessment – Follow-up

Who do you conduct follow-up calls with?
(Select all that apply)

Promoters

Passives

Detractors

How frequently do teams meet to review customer feedback and set priority actions and accountability for improving customer experience outcomes

Daily

Weekly

Monthly

Quarterly

We do not meet regularly

217

# Where do I start?

You are then asked with whom you follow up, what proportion of Detractors receive a follow-up call and what proportion of those get the call within 48 hours. That is followed by a question on the frequency of meetings to follow up on customer feedback. These dialogs are in Exhibit 12.4.

The assessment goes on to look at employee training and your approach to employee surveys as shown in Exhibit 12.5.

## Exhibit 12.5

Employee training and surveys

What percentage of your employees would you estimate can explain NPS. why the company feels it is important and what is truly required to delight customers and improve NPS?

| <20% | 20-40% | 41-60% | 61-80% | 81-100% |

How frequently do you capture employee advocacy data and feedback?
(Select all that apply.)

We conduct an annual employee survey

We conduct 2-4 employee surveys per year

We conduct monthly surveys

We conduct weekly pulse check surveys

We do not conduct employee surveys

There is a final question on whether you have someone who spends more than 60% of their time working on the Net Promoter System. You then get your color-coded framework shown in Exhibit 12.6, followed by a table that gives you a short summary of what loyalty leaders do in each area, shown in Exhibit 12.7.

## Exhibit 12.6

Bain self-assessment summary

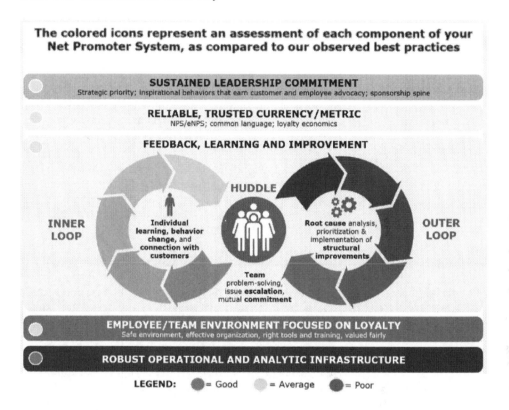

The colored icons represent an assessment of each component of your Net Promoter System, as compared to our observed best practices

**SUSTAINED LEADERSHIP COMMITMENT**
Strategic priority; inspirational behaviors that earn customer and employee advocacy; sponsorship spine

**RELIABLE, TRUSTED CURRENCY/METRIC**
NPS/eNPS; common language; loyalty economics

**FEEDBACK, LEARNING AND IMPROVEMENT**

HUDDLE

INNER LOOP

Individual learning, behavior change, and connection with customers

Team problem-solving, issue escalation, mutual commitment

Root cause analysis, prioritization & implementation of structural improvements

OUTER LOOP

**EMPLOYEE/TEAM ENVIRONMENT FOCUSED ON LOYALTY**
Safe environment, effective organization, right tools and training, valued fairly

**ROBUST OPERATIONAL AND ANALYTIC INFRASTRUCTURE**

LEGEND: ● = Good  ● = Average  ● = Poor

Overall, this is an excellent way to evaluate progress on an NPS improvement journey, providing you have already started. The graphic is useful for presentations, and the table gives you talking points. If you have only started your NPS implementation in the last couple of years, you may not have anything that is green yet. As already advised when discussing communication, I would not use the graphic outside the implementation team if you have more than one red status item. If your assessment has a lot of red, I recommend changing the color scale and legend. Make 'Good' blue, 'Average' green, and 'Poor' yellow.

## Exhibit 12.7

Bain loyalty leader characteristics

| System Component | Characteristics displayed by loyalty leaders |
|---|---|
| Sustained Leadership and Commitment | Senior executives focus **attention on customer issues**; make regular **time to interact with customers**; establish clearly defined, **compelling vision** for the future; **set inspiring but achievable goals** for Competitive NPS leadership. |
| Reliable, Trusted Currency/Metric | Leading companies frequently and **consistently measure** NPS; ensure **high response rates** for core customer segments; actively **eliminate gaming** and other biases; validate **linkage between scores and actual customer behavior** and economics |
| Feedback, Learning and Improvement | Leading companies rapidly **close the loop** with any customer whose feedback indicates it is merited; **share customer feedback** directly with employees; conduct regular **team huddles & individual coaching** sessions to grow capabilities; **analyze feedback** & root causes; escalate **& prioritize key cross-functional issues** |
| Employee/Team Environment Focused on Loyalty | Employees receive **sufficient training and coaching** on the processes and behaviors required to support the Net Promoter System; KPIs and **metrics counter to the NPS mission are avoided** or actively eliminated; **NPS improvement targets** are set for each BU/product line/team |
| Robust Operational and Analytical Infastructure | Leading companies staff a robust **Advocacy Team**; have data & **analytical support**; use **integrated survey, CRM and Financial systems**; leverage closed loop **workflow & reporting systems** |

220

# 13.    Conclusion

# 13.1 The final word

The Net Promoter System is simple in principle, and sophisticated in practice. Success requires all five elements of the framework to be implemented comprehensively and to be communicated clearly. As it is the most successful customer experience improvement system on the planet, a lot of advice is available. The quality is variable, and a substantial part of the advice comes from people who are trying to sell proprietary solutions. Advice suggesting NPS is not a good system tends to come from people selling an alternative. I have used a lot of different systems over my career, and feel my views are unbiased. Yes, it is possible to come up with more complex metrics that are better revenue predictors. Yes, it is possible to come up with different improvement methodologies that are equivalent to the framework developed by Bain and used for this book. I believe the relative simplicity of both the metric and the framework make the Net Promoter System far easier to communicate, and therefore far easier to implement, than any other system I have seen. I hope the advice and experience I have shared here will accelerate your implementation journey.

# Learning check answers

# Answers

Introduction
1. True.
2. False. Other questions finished at the top of the list for a few industries. The recommendation question finished just behind in those cases.
3. False. The scale can also go from ten to zero, or indeed one to five. It is important to be consistent, using a single scale for your company and keeping it the same from survey to survey.
4. True.
5. False. While *The Ultimate Question 2.0* is a reference source, it has been updated extensively. The Bain updates to the system are covered in the Net Promoter System Podcasts. Satmetrix has independently developed what it calls NPS2.

Reliable trusted metric — Part 1
1. False. What matters is the trend relative to competition. If your number is higher and has stayed flat, but your competitor's number has improved, they will take share from you in the future.
2. False. A good NPS score is one whose trend is better than the trend of your main competitor. A world-class score is one that is better than the competition and improving faster. The absolute number has no importance.
3. True. You may want to treat a single outlier result as suspicious if the sample size is smaller than for your other competitors or countries, for example. However, if you see similar numbers in sequential sampling periods, you should trust the trend.
4. True, though the survey vendors also supply demographic data so you can do your own weighting if you so wish. However, when

vendors such as Temkin publish tables on their websites, there is no weighting.

## Reliable trusted metric — Part 2

1. True. Using a serif font like Times New Roman in emails improves response rates compared to using a non-serif font like Arial.
2. False. You should only survey if you have the people, funding and plans to act on the input.
3. True, at least in the author's experiments. There are software vendors who say that it triples response rates.
4. False. Do your best to make all competitive comparisons local. Comparing NPS scores between countries is not helpful.
5. True, and the effect is substantial. You can only consider an NPS survey to be truly representative of the customer population when you have response rates above about 50%. Such numbers are rare for transactional surveys, another reason to be selective when using them.
6. False. The longer your survey questionnaire, the more people will drop out before completing it. Compared to a 3-question survey, about 6% of the people who start a 20-question survey will not complete it, rising to 10% for a 40-question survey.

## Reliable trusted metric — Part 3

1. True. Renewing a contract is mainly an administrative effort and costs far less than hunting for and acquiring a new customer.
2. False. You need to do the analysis for each part of your business for which you produce a P&L.
3. True. This is to do with the average purchase cycle. Even if they love you, people are relatively unlikely to buy the same thing again right away. This varies widely by type of product.
4. False. Promoters tend to get lower discounts than less happy customers and discounts from list prices are not in your P&L in most accounting systems.
5. False. You need to distinguish between customers who spend a lot and those who don't spend much on your type of product or service when calculating lifetime value. Large spenders tend to be more

demanding than small spenders, and therefore tend to give lower NPS scores.

## Feedback, learning and improvement
1. True, and the Huddle is a place where you can work on the intersection between the two, for example when an item comes up frequently in the Inner Loop and needs to be addressed more systematically.
2. False. You need to prioritize. Come up with your own prioritization criteria. For example, you could decide that items that come up more frequently from your largest, or perhaps your newest customers should have a higher priority.

## Robust operational and analytic infrastructure
1. False. It does not matter much where the customer experience leader reports, within reason. Ideally the Chief Customer Officer should report to the CEO. If they report more than one layer down, they are unlikely to be effective. In the specific case of Marketing, Marketing oversees a small subset of the many touchpoints that affect a customer, and is one potential choice for a reporting line. The author recommends reporting to the corporate Chief of Staff, if there is one, and you need to have the person report a layer down.
2. True. Humans are the best single solution, but cannot deal with high volumes. They also need to be trained to minimize bias and ensure consistency. The best results come from combining software screening with final human analysis.

## Employee/Team environment focused on loyalty
1. False. Surprisingly, it does not matter much for the average business. There are high-touch businesses like restaurants where it seems to matter a lot.
2. True. The principles and methodology are almost identical for internal use.
3. True, as of August 2017.

# Learning check answers

Sustained leadership commitment
1   True. Unfortunately, human brains don't work as rationally as we may like to think, so starting with numbers tends to be ineffective. You need to lead with something that addresses emotional and intuitive thinking. Engage rational thought afterwards.
2   False. Executive Sponsors should understand the customer's industry and have a personal interest in the area.

# Index

Made in the USA
Lexington, KY
20 November 2017